What others are saying about
Six Ways to Keep the "Good" in Your Boy

"Dannah Gresh has done a fabulous job addressing many of the issues that concern our boys. I highly recommend her insights, biblical instruction, and practical mom application. These pages are marching orders! It's time to fight for the good in our boys!"

—ANGELA THOMAS,
bestselling author and speaker

"With two young sons of our own, Jean and I can certainly attest to the challenges raising boys can bring! Dannah and Bob offer parents a fascinating look into the development of tween and teen boys, as well as a wealth of practical, hands-on musts for successfully connecting with them. Learn the 'how-to's' for building and strengthening parent/son relationships and guiding young men toward a purposeful, God-honoring adulthood."

—JIM DALY, president,
Focus on the Family

"*Six Ways to Keep the 'Good' in Your Boy* provides valuable information and points out positive ways to channel all that testosterone-induced male energy. If you have a boy, this is a book you must read!"

—MARY A. KASSIAN,
author, *Girls Gone Wise*

"Every mom wants her little boy to grow to be a caring and courageous man. The truth is, she can either be his ally on that journey to manhood, or she can hinder his progress. Thankfully, Dannah Gresh has sound, practical wisdom for moms who want their sons to be the men God made them to be."

—BOB LEPINE,
co-host of *FamilyLife Today*

Six Ways to Keep the "Good" in Your Boy

Dannah Gresh

HARVEST HOUSE PUBLISHERS
EUGENE, OREGON

Cover by Garborg Design Works, Savage, Minnesota

Cover photo © Dmitriy Shironosov / Shutterstock

SIX WAYS TO KEEP THE "GOOD" IN YOUR BOY
Copyright © 2012 by Dannah and Bob Gresh
Published by Harvest House Publishers
Eugene, Oregon 97402
www.harvesthousepublishers.com

Library of Congress Cataloging-in-Publication Data
    Gresh, Dannah.
    Six ways to keep the "good" in your boy / Dannah Gresh.
        p. cm.
    ISBN 978-0-7369-4579-0 (pbk.)
    ISBN 978-0-7369-4580-6 (eBook)
    1. Mothers and sons—Religious aspects—Christianity. 2. Child rearing—Religious aspects—Christianity. 3. Sons—Religious life. I. Title.
    BV4529.18.G745 2012
    248.8'45—dc23
                                                                    2011030820

Printed in the United States of America

15 16 17 18 19 20 / VP-SK / 10 9 8 7 6

*To my dear friend
Jackie Stauffer, who
raised a good son to
be friends with mine*

A Good Word for Their Goodness Goes to...

Like most books, this one wasn't written alone. There were a lot of people expressing their love to me in the form of goodness as defined in this book. Thanks to...

Kelly Nebel, who was the first to do any work on this book. She is a research geek. (Takes one to know one.) She rolled up her sleeves and is the reason that this book communicates intelligently! In the middle of this she got married. May she and Mark produce many good boys!

Suzie Rothgeb, who followed God's heart to offer to edit. While we were in the middle of writing this book, God spoke to Bob and me about resting and tending to our own family. How would I do that with a book to edit and a deadline to meet? Suzie e-mailed me out of the blue and asked if she could help. What an answer to prayer and what a great editor! The Christian publishing industry has just found its next great critical thinker!

Harvest House Publishers, who just makes me feel so welcomed. While I was writing this, Terry Glaspey and Larae Weikert actually trekked out to central Pennsylvania and we had some stimulating conversations about how to craft critical pieces of this message. What a treasure that day was. Paul Gossard, editor extraordinaire, made certain that our thinking actually did make sense. Thank you for the privilege of partnering with you.

The Resource Agency, who helps me strategically plan my writing ministry. Mike Keil has become such a dear friend to Bob and me. It did not go without notice that as I worked on this, Mike and his wife, Tina, launched a very good son into married life. Congratulations, Jason and Lillian!

Eileen King, my assistant, who is so notably full of goodness that I would not survive writing deadlines without her. Thank you for making my life more manageable and organized.

But mostly, thanks goes to my family: Bob, who wrote this one with me. Lexi and Autumn, for patience when your mom had a deadline to meet. And especially, Robby Gresh. I've been thankful to God for him from the moment I first held him. His goodness humbles me every day.

Contents

Part Two: Six Ways to Keep the "Good" in Your Boy

Foreword

by Rob Gresh

<hr>

A few months ago, I received an e-mail from my mom with the manuscript of this book attached, asking me to look it over and make sure I was okay with everything she shares about me. I read it through and then replied, "It's really good and you make me look pretty good, so you can keep everything." She then replied, "I don't make anybody look good. You *are* good. I'm proud of you."

This may not seem that significant to you, but it meant a lot to me. My mom is always encouraging me, whether through an occasional text or e-mail or a basket full of snacks during finals week. That said, my parents have never been afraid to tell me when I can do better, and they have always delivered those messages with love.

When I was younger, I thought I had the best parents in the world. I assumed that all kids must feel the same way about theirs. As I grew older I realized that my relationship with my mom and dad was special. Other kids often didn't share the love and respect with their parents that I share with mine. And I think that most students in college can identify a few things that they would like to do differently with their kids than their parents did with them. When my mom asked me what I wish she and dad had done differently, I honestly couldn't think of anything significant. My parents aren't perfect, and they wouldn't want me to tell you that they are, but I really feel they are incredible. They set a great example for me every day. They encourage me. They know the difference between "you're doing it all wrong" and "you can do better." And most important, they have always made it clear that they love me. I'm not sure what I could do differently, but I will be thrilled if I am as good a parent to my kids as my parents are to me.

Will reading this book help you become a better parent? Only if a personal training session with Michael Jordan will make you a better basketball player. (That means, *Absolutely*!) So read it and apply what you learn, and your son will thank you later. He might even write you a nice foreword one day.

Rob Gresh

Introducing the Six Ways

by Bob Gresh

My first memory of being a dad is of swaddling up my son. I would wrap him so tightly that the blankets could not possibly come loose. Then I'd put his tiny head in the palm of my hand and place his body along my forearm so his bum and tightly wrapped tootsies were right at my elbow. I carried him one-handed, just like I did the football when I played flag football in high school.

I'm not sure that's the proper way to hold a baby.

I could've given so much more confident advice to fathers before I was one. When Dannah and I were still dating we dreamed about being great parents. Ours would be the home where all the kids wanted to hang out. And it was, but the reality show of our lives is so much more twisty-turny, complicated, heart-wrenching…and I should add, ultimately joyful…than I could have ever imagined. It was surprising to find out just how much salt was needed to go with the words I'd eventually eat.

But that's kind of been the story of our lives. Dannah and I are ordinary people who have made a lot of common mistakes in the journey of life. If you've read any of her books, you know that a particular passion in our lives is to encourage the church to live in purity and to experience marriage as a picture of Christ and his bride, the church. Sadly, these two things are under attack from the enemy, and the church often looks more like a bloodied soldier than a beautiful bride. Dannah and I have been no exception.

I made it to my wedding bed a virgin. Sadly, I did not make it there pure. And you might be surprised how old I was when the enemy swooped in to start the battle of my life.

I remember the day well, though it happened over 30 years ago. The attic was thick with heat. Dust particles floated in the rays of the sun that slipped through the rafters. I could smell mothballs. My mind reeled with confusion.

I'd stumbled onto a magazine. One quick glance at the cover enticed me to look inside. A desire was awakened that I'd never known before. So I looked. I looked at her. She was beautiful. Naked. Curvy. I wanted so very much to look—so why was everything in me screaming "No"?

I could never have imagined that anything that looked so good could make me feel so bad.

I was 12.

This battle became ongoing. No one told me what do to with it, so I lost it for a long time. Until someone began to walk beside me and teach me how to win.

Today the Internet insidiously seeks to introduce our sons—yours and mine—to this same battle, but much earlier. And there are other battles: aggressive girls, emasculation by our culture, and the rising prevalence of ADD in boys, to name a few. We have to be ready to help our boys win.

We'd like to help you do just that!

Dannah and I have made it a core value of our ministry to never write or speak about something we haven't yet lived out. We refused to write about raising tweens, teens, or young men and women until we'd been through the stage. That was one of the best decisions of our lives.

Our son is now just about ready to launch into his young adult life. This year, he will graduate from college and search for his first job. Frankly, Robby was easy to raise. He came out compliant, with a heart to please others. The other day Dannah overheard his teenaged sister Lexi telling someone about him. "He's just good. He's as good a person as you will ever meet!"

And so he is.

I think we can write to you with some credibility about how to keep the good in your boy. We've done it. (But remember, he *came out* compliant. We can't take all the credit, nor would we try. And we don't want you to think your strong-willed boy can be anything less than good.) With God's help and his daily patience with us, we have achieved something we greatly desired—something you too probably desire if you're reading this book.

Speaking of this book, I'm writing my parts of this book upon a pressing deadline. That's the only way those of us with ADD (attention deficit disorder) can do it. Extreme pressure creates extreme focus. You'll notice that the sections and chapters that I write are a bit…well, variant…in topic. They're also funnier because—if you have an ADD boy, you know we're entertaining! (Can I just put a word in to say that even someone with ADD can be "good"? You haven't failed as a parent because other kids sit so quietly, do their homework without excessive parental reminders, and then remember to hand it in! We've included a special appendix just for those of you whose battles are made more interesting because of ADD. But know this: *Your* son can be "good"!)

> ### *Click here*
> When you see the words "Click Here," it's time to go online and discover a great resource! Go to your favorite place to buy books and check out these two comprehensive books on raising boys. They may be helpful if that's something you're looking for.
>
> - *Bringing Up Boys* by Dr. James Dobson
> - *Boys Should Be Boys: 7 Secrets to Raising Healthy Sons* by Dr. Meg Meeker

I also write with humility. The point of this book is the biblical goal of instilling goodness into your boy. Even though we've raised our son to be good, he is just starting his perilous journey as a man. He's got a lot of years to live it out. I'm mindful of that as I write about him with gratefulness and a father's heart of pride.

Dannah and I will make this promise to you as we write: We will admit the mistakes we made and the regrets we have, for there are so many things we would have done differently. So many places we failed.

So many times I compared myself to that mythical perfect father. Actually, he's apparently not mythical—he's been well documented in many parenting books through the years. I crumbled when I read books describing fathers who never missed a night of praying for their child… or praying on their knees with their child each day…or for 20 years before they were born. Oh, how I wish I could have done that! How I wish I had responded with biblical patience each time my aggravation level exceeded my ability to respond with a life-changing Bible verse or at least a quote from C.S. Lewis, Augustine, or even the founder of Chick-fil-A.

I am flawed.

And just as important, I am unique. After all, did Augustine ever surprise his kids with a pet peacock? Or dive into a baptismal pool and tear his Achilles?

I'll bet not.

After all, Augustine didn't even have kids. (Picture me smiling.)

If you're a mom reading this book, you may be wondering what you've gotten yourself into now that we've met. Well, after *Six Ways to Keep the "Little" in Your Girl* scratched an itch that moms just couldn't reach, Dannah was asked to pen this book on raising tween boys. As she began the process she quickly realized two things.

First, it takes a man to raise a boy. (My wife is smart!) So she asked me to join her on this project so that you can confidently hand this book to your man. He will be able to trust what's written here because it's been approved by someone who knows that a Hail Mary is not just something you pray if you're a Catholic, and that a Fu Manchu is something you grow on your face. These are important qualifications when you're taking advice from someone about manhood. So, in between Dannah's great research and expertise, you'll get a good dose of me and my ADD whims. (Watch for sidebars and Random Bob Thoughts, which show up looking like Post-It notes on the pages.)

Random Bob Thought:
If you want to get your man to read this with you, don't ask him! Instead, tell him some guy with ADD is writing about Hail Mary's and Fu Manchu's and you need help translating.

Second, a lot of you won't have a man with which you can share this book. More important, you don't have a man who can share in raising your boy. While Dannah's book on raising girls didn't create as great a need for the wisdom of a single mom, this one does. So Dannah called Angela Thomas, who is a nationally known speaker and the author of several bestselling books, including *My Single Mom Life*. My wife spent some time with her yesterday afternoon and she's in love with her. She came home in that excited "I-just-spent-a-lot-of-time-getting-revved-up-by-girlfriend-talk-so-sit-down-and-let-me-tell-you-every-detail" mood. I have a feeling that if you don't already love Angela Thomas, you will by the end of this book—single mom or not.

And hopefully, you'll still like me too!

So, let's get on to the task of keeping the "good" in our boys.

A few things you should know about
Six Ways to Keep the "Good" in Your Boy
by Dannah Gresh

1. This book is not meant to be a comprehensive overview of parenting boys...or even parenting tween boys. My area of study is primarily in the field of sexuality and purity and related topics. What I hope to bring to your parenting toolbox is specific skills to raise a tween boy to become a pure man of integrity and honor. I'll introduce the "six ways" that make this achievable and give you specific, creative ideas to introduce them.

2. If you're a mom, you're the person I'm writing this book for. I'm seeking to help you strengthen your mother–son relationship, specifically during the years just preceding adolescence. These are really important years for your relationship with your son, and I'll share a lot of ideas for how a mother can affirm a boy's entrance into manhood.

But what makes writing this book so terribly challenging is that it takes a man to build a man. A father's role becomes more critical during the tween years. As I've written this book, I've been careful to include tips, with Bob's help, on how you can encourage your son's dad—even if he is not your spouse. While I won't cover the father–son relationship in depth, I do want you to have an understanding of how your relationship with your son intersects with the one he'll have with his dad.

3. The research in this book is scientifically valid no matter what your belief system is, but I'll write from a Judeo–Christian perspective. I can't really separate my advice in parenting from my own personal goal to raise children who make choices that are in conformity to God's written standard of truth, the Bible. That will be apparent as I write, but many of the thinkers who have shaped my parenting in the area of honor, integrity, and purity would be considered "far left" politically and perhaps secular humanist in their worldview. I respect them and they've brought great insight to my parenting. When it comes to raising boys who will be good men, we can find a lot of common ground. I hope you'll find that to be true as you read this, even if you don't share my perspective on life.

4. There are exceptions to many things I write in this book. For example, when I say that most tween and teen boys desperately need physical activity outside to release all the aggression that testosterone creates, I mean just that. *Most!* Not all. Throughout the book, I'll be letting you know what the norms are in terms of readiness for talking to your son about sex, or introducing him to dangers on the Internet. I might suggest a parenting skill that will help him to clarify his sense of purpose—very important for boys—or deal with his obsession with gaming, but that doesn't mean it's going to work for your child. Every child is unique. There are also boys who need special individual care and counseling. So please don't use this book as a fail-proof answer to your son's needs.

5. The goal of this book is not to guarantee your son's purity, integrity, and sense of honor, but to help you to be faithful to do your part to protect those things. I'm not writing a "how-to" guide where we use canned rules and step-by-step instructions to create a generation of legalistically raised super-sons. There exists no single set of parenting methods that guarantee a specific outcome. It is ultimately through God's grace that the values of purity and self-respect have been crafted into our son, Robby. But God gave him to us with the expectation we would teach him moral values that help him to be physically, emotionally, and spiritually whole.

With that responsibility in mind, we studied the work of respected family teachers like Dennis and Barbara Rainey, Dr. James Dobson, Tim and Beverly LaHaye, and even the work of some non-Christian thinkers like Michael Gurian and Dr. Edward Hallowell. I wanted to consistently apply sound principles in the moral development of all three of our children, and I'm delighted with the results. Bob and I feel like faithful parents. If this book helps you achieve that, it will have done its job.

6. Faithful parents still must often apply grace to children who don't embrace moral values. I can't promise that putting everything in this book into practice will guarantee that your son will be a self-sacrificing, community-minded, and porn-free teenager. The Reverend Billy Graham had a son, Franklin, who rebelled hard as a young man. (Thankfully, as an adult he's walking with the Lord and is at the helm of the Samaritan's Purse organization.) Faithful parents often find themselves aching over their children's struggles or outright defiance. You see, rebellion has existed since the beginning of time where, amid the perfect paradise of the Garden of Eden, two that walked with a perfect Father rejected his ways. Since then we haven't stopped repeatedly turning away from his goodness.

Therefore, be ready at all stages of parenting to give grace. Just as your 2-year-old threw a fit in public and needed grace, your 16-year-old may create a scene that needs much grace. Ultimately, that's what our Father God does for us each day, isn't it?

Part One

Becoming a Connecting Mom

Before we dig into the Six Ways to Keep the "Good" in Your Boy, you and I are going to explore some biological facts and fundamental truths that will be a starting point for understanding how to connect with your son in a deeper way. These first few chapters are similar to the beginning chapters in *Six Ways to Keep the "Little" in Your Girl*. Please don't skip them. They are full of intriguing research about your son's brain and body chemicals—something a mom can hardly wrap her female brain around! I've also thrown in ideas for funky activities to do with your son.

But foundational to my philosophy laid out in the next several chapters is the verse below. You might want to post it somewhere, like in your bathroom or on your fridge, so you can hide it away in your heart. As you'll see, goodness is something God wants all of us to pursue!

> Do not be overcome by evil,
> but overcome evil with good.
>
> ROMANS 12:21

"I'm concerned that boys today lack respect for girls and for those in authority over them. They are not taking responsibility for their actions and what is required of them as men. They tend to want to please themselves and not be concerned with others, especially when it comes to work. They do not have a good work ethic."

Linda, mother of Robert, 19

CHAPTER 1

Is There a Mouse in That Cookie Box?

A box of cookies and a dead mouse.

The combination conjures up one of the proudest memories of mothering my wonderful son, Robby. (If you meet him, you can call him Rob. But I can't. He's still *my* Robby even if he's the size of a linebacker.) He was a freshman at Grace Prep high school and was just returning from a school-assigned Random Act of Kindness when these two mismatched objects—mouse and cookies—mingled together to create an equally odd mixture of emotions.

Just hours earlier, armed with nothing more than a few boxes of cookies and several rakes, he and a few friends had set out to do some good. They'd come back a little flustered, but laughing their experience off like four cool 15-year-old boys should.

"We just got yelled at," said Robby, wearing the words like a badge of courage.

"By whom?" I asked.

"Some crazy woman who thought there must be a mouse in the cookies we were trying to give her," he answered defensively.

"What!" I was just a little aggravated, having been the one who had issued the assignment. How could anyone react with anger and suspicion (particularly in our small, friendly town) to a box of cookies and an offer to do yard work? Surely they must have misunderstood. "Tell me what happened. Play-by-play," I said.

"Well, we knocked on the lady's door to give her the cookies and ask permission to rake her leaves," Robby answered. "When we tried to hand her the cookies she looked afraid and angrily said, 'Is there a dead mouse in that box?'"

> **Goodness**
> [*good*-nis] "the state or quality of being good; a euphemism for God"
> —*actual definition found at dictionary.com*

The other boys snickered. I could see that they thought it was funny, but that it also bothered them.

I was having a hard time believing it.

"We promised there wasn't a mouse in there, but she just couldn't believe we were there to do anything good. So one of the guys said, 'Look, we just want to show you God's love in a practical way.'"

This made me smile. It was what they'd been taught. "Transfer the credit of this good act to God," I'd said in class.

"What'd she say when you said that?" I asked.

"She grabbed the cookies, said, 'Rake if you want to,' and slammed the door in our faces!" said Robby. "So, we raked."

I could tell that the guys were still a bit shaken, and I was a bit angry that they hadn't been met with the reward of a simple "thank you."

A few weeks later, God brought the whole thing full circle with a letter that came in the mail. One of the members of Robby's group got to read it out loud in chapel. I wish I still had it. It went something like this:

> *Dear Grace Prep:*
>
> *Recently some boys from your school came here to deliver cookies to my daughter and me. They also raked our leaves. I'm embarrassed to say that I didn't trust them. I am sorry. (For the record, they were really yummy cookies.)*

I think God sent those boys here.

You see, my husband—my daughter's father—died recently and it has been tough. Just that morning my daughter and I kind of put a test out there for God. We prayed, saying, "If you're really there and you really see us, show up!"

When he did, we didn't recognize him right away. But I have no doubt that God sent those high-school boys to remind us that he sees us.

Thank you.

You could have heard a pin drop in that room of high-school kids when the letter was read. We were all simply struck with the power of goodness.

But here's why this wonderful memory not only floods my heart with pride, but also makes me sad: *We've lost our faith in the goodness of boys and men*. And not wholly without reason.

Where Have All the Good Men Gone?

A title of a recent *Wall Street Journal* article inquired, "Where Have the Good Men Gone?" A current Amazon bestseller seeks to answer the question, *Is There Anything Good About Men?* Since the 2004 coining of the word "adultescent,"[1] we've had something to call the young adult male who is so busy playing Call of Duty on his PlayStation 4 that he has no real-life call of duty. No honor. No integrity. No goodness. Just a seventh-grade mind-set and responsibility level trapped in the flabby body of an adult who often still lives at home or in a tacky bachelor pad with other adultescents. The phenomenon is what caused Kay S. Hymowitz to pen the book *Manning Up*, in which she writes,

> *Not so long ago, average mid-twentysomethings, both male and female, had achieved most of the milestones of adulthood: high school diploma, financial independence, marriage, and children. These days [the males] hang out in a novel sort of limbo, a hybrid state of semi-hormonal adolescence and responsible self-reliance.*[2]

High-school English teacher Joe Carmichiel has written a book entitled *Permanent Adolescence: Why Boys Don't Grow Up,* because "a large number of today's teenagers, especially boys, see no reason to accept or pursue adulthood since it is of so little value to the larger culture."[3] So, with no motivation to *do* anything, many of these young men remain in a state of wimpy complacency well into their twenties, even thirties.

Along with this state of immaturity that many boys will embrace as they grow older is a culturally acceptable pressure for boys to be bad—both complacent and void of character. By the time a boy is finished with high school, he is likely to have three crucial areas of character ripped right out of him:

1. Over 50 percent of young men will have become sexually active in a casual-sex culture where they're likely to have an average of 9.7 sexual partners before they graduate from college.[4] (There goes his purity.)

2. Most of them will be exposed to porn as a tween or early teen, with the median age of first exposure being about 11. This catapults many of them into a world of double-mindedness where they are one boy at home and in public—and another entirely in their private world. (There goes his integrity.)

3. Many will have succumbed to an emasculated version of manhood that strips them of their drive to be leaders and protectors who do good. (There goes his honor.)

Our boys need to be taught to grow up.
And to be good.

While *Six Ways to Keep the "Little" in Your Girl* cried out for us to band together against the culture's pressure for our little girls to grow up too fast, this book pleads with you to join us in raising sons who are prepared to embrace the responsibility of growing up.

It's been our goal to create a character base for our son to be a man of integrity, honor, and purity. Bob and I want him to be good. Fortunately, our life work led me into the depths of research, and I learned that we had to start building a foundation for our son to rise to the call of manhood…when he was still just our "good boy"! Raising a son to reflect your value system when he is a man is—in part—a matter of introducing those values to him in an age-appropriate manner when he is a *tween*. Social science offers us statistical lines of footprints showing how a boy will turn out based on what he is exposed to and when. Sadly, our boys have got a tough battle ahead. It's been a long time since they've seen anything but "adultescent" or "bad" examples of manhood dominating our culture.

Why Are Boys "Bad"?

Robert Coles, a pioneer in the field of moral intelligence, brings clarity to the definition *badness* when he writes,

> *Bad boys display a "heightened destructive self-absorption, in all its melancholy stages." In essence, we go bad when "we lose sight of our obligation to others."*[5]

Badness is not simply the loss of innocence, purity, integrity, and honor, but also the loss of vision to see the needs of others and to act on them. It's a complacent, self-absorbed lifestyle that is void of character.

I think we have a bad-boy mentality in our culture for two primary reasons.

The first reason boys become bad is that the feminist movement has told us they are *bad.* Michael Gurian, author of *The Wonder of Boys*, though seeming to embrace the feminist movement as a whole, points out a few devastating myths it introduced to convince our boys that they are "bad." Here are two that resonate with me:

> *Myth Number One: "that masculinity is responsible for the world's ills and femininity is the world's salvation."*[6]
>
> *Myth Number Two: "males destroy, females create; males*

*stand in the way of positive spiritual/social values; males
are inherently violent."[7]*

While a deeper study of the feminist movement would betray an
agenda to introduce these fallacies, we don't have to get that academic
to see how much we are influenced to believe these myths in our politically correct culture.

Just consider how prevalently they are portrayed in the media. Television alone reinforces them. *Two and a Half Men*, "the biggest hit comedy
of the past decade" according to the *New York Times*, features a hedo-
nist formerly played by Charlie Sheen. After eight seasons, the show
was stalled when Sheen went into rehab for drug use. He was then fired
for making disparaging remarks about the show's producers. On and
off screen he was self-absorbed and void of character. Other shows display the contrast of the valuable female to the valueless male. Reruns
of *The Simpsons* portray Lisa as bright and beautiful and Bart as out of
shape and selfish. Co-ed television commercials often portray the guy
as a doofus and the girl as smart. It's funny. It really is. But how much
of it can we expose ourselves to before we believe it? And that takes me
to my next concern.

*The second reason boys are "bad" is that they have become what has been
expected of them, just like any individual tends to fulfill what has been
prophesied about them.* Of course, they've had help from their parents (or
lack thereof), their culture (and its emasculation), their economy (and
its consumeristic "me" mentality), and their churches (who haven't
done much to stand against the feminist untruths). But today's men as
a whole have pretty much rolled over and taken it.

It's probably a good idea for me, Bob, to step in here. I'm a guy. If
anyone's going to throw us under the bus, it should be me. It has always
befuddled me that the prettiest, nicest girls are always attracted to the
bad boys. From the jock who bullies everyone at school to the kid in a
leather jacket who doles out drugs after school, nice girls often go after
the bad boys. In the Twilight series, bad boy Edward Cullen makes good
girl Bella Swan swoon. In real life, the stars live out the scenario. Kevin

Federline was the top bad boy of the tabloids when he nabbed the most famous girl on the planet at the height of her career, Britney Spears. Katy Perry, former Christian music artist gone sexual tease, pledged herself to bad boy Russell Brand.

I think that the constant drip of these scenarios into our spirits makes us want to be bad boys. Let's be real: A guy desires a beautiful girl, and while the ones in the headlines might not be all that chaste, they're often *portrayed* as the good girl taken by the bad boy. And guess what? Guys want nice girls. So, we begin to believe that maybe we're supposed to be bad.

And if we're not, we're boring.

Come on. The media glorifies the bad boys—from *Grease*'s Danny Zuko to *Pirates of the Caribbean*'s Captain Jack Sparrow—not the plain-vanilla good guys. I didn't watch this show, but Dannah says *Gilmore Girls* played to this big time when Rory fell for beautiful boy Dean *until* bad boy Jess came to town. The bad boy is so often the one the girl wants and celebrates.

Click here!

Go to oellerslie.com/intercession .html (on the ministry website of authors and speakers Eric and Leslie Ludy) to see a fantastic, motivating short film (seven and a half minutes) on the role of intercession in raising up good boys.

"One of the key definitions of Christianity could be is a man or woman who…is made strong. Why? So that they are *useful* to God and they are not just constantly inwardly fighting demons. They can be outward-focused." —Eric Ludy

Conversely, there aren't a lot of movies being made about Billy Graham, the kid who called 9-1-1 and delivered his mom's baby, or the apostle Paul. These are true heroes…but they're good. And good is boring, according to movie producers. Since no one rises up to celebrate the good, most guys—though innately built to be conquerors—roll over and become boring.

In some twisted place in our minds, we'd much rather be bad than boring because that's how you get the girl. But many of us are afraid of being the real bad boy. So we just get complacent. We roll over and stay in some limbo—a state of in-between. Not really bad. Not really good. Or so we think.

In reality, *this complacency is the absolute root of badness*.

The Tree

Complacency was at the root of the first bad move among men. (Yes—*the* bad move of all time.) Adam had the most complacent moment of all when he stood at the foot of the Tree of the Knowledge of Good and Evil. It was Eve who wore the pants in the first family during this cat-astrophic moment. She took the lead and reached for the fruit of the Tree. Adam just got all quiet, passive and...well, boring. The Scriptures don't note that he was deceived, tempted, or lied to like Eve. Just that he went along with it.

Some theologians believe that there was something in the way that Eve was crafted which made her more vulnerable to deception. (Just consider how often we women are prone to think things like "I'm fat!" Haven't seen too many guys obsessing over that thought. Or maybe you've been prone to believe the lie "No one really likes me." Men don't struggle with that as often or as easily. Women are just prone to believ-ing lies.) However, many believe that Satan approached Eve because he was attempting to throw over the created order by getting her to take leadership over her husband. And Adam seemed to passively accept this evil situation to gratify his flesh. Sounds a bit too much like many men of today.

Complacency led to the first sin. (Perhaps, had Adam chosen to speak truth to Eve, he could have led her away from that horrible orig-inal sin.) His failure to lead changed the course of history. We believe that the same kind of complacency that showed itself at the foot of the Tree still leads men to badness.

Goodness vs. Badness

While a bad boy's greatest desire is to live according to his desires, a good boy, according to Robert Coles, has an outward focus:

> *Good…boys…have learned to take seriously the very notion,*
> *the desirability of goodness—living up to the Golden Rule.* [8]

The Greek word for *goodness* (used in our take-to-heart verse, Romans 12:21) appears in the New Testament in three forms, all of which are rooted in the Hebrew word *tod*, which means "usefulness" or "beneficialness." Are we bringing up boys who understand their call of duty to be useful contributors to society, to be beneficial to others?

Goodness is the quality that makes us put others ahead of ourselves. It's the moral compass that keeps the world safe, happy, and working. It's the drive that makes us want to function in families rather than isolation. It's the internal road sign that takes us away from our own desires and toward the destiny of meeting the needs of others. Without it, we are "bad." That's probably why all of us—male and female—are called to goodness.

> *Do not be overcome by evil,*
> *but overcome evil with good.*
> Romans 12:21

God *is* good

The ultimate reason we must raise our boys to be good is that it reflects the character of God. His goodness is a bedrock truth of Scripture and is inseparable from his nature. If we are to be a picture of him, we must possess goodness. He is good not only in a general sense, but he is good *to* us and *for* us. This element of his character expresses his selflessness and desire to exist on behalf of others. When people are good, they act *toward* and *for* others, as opposed to losing sight of others as their own needs and desires consume them.

The greatest societal pressure is "athletes, movie stars, politicians who exemplify and condone bad behavior."

Shirley, mother of grown sons
David, Steve, and Mark

CHAPTER 2

A Mom's Greatest Fears

C ould I get a few moments alone with you?" asked a friend.

"How about now?" I answered, sensing the heaviness of her heart.

Her son was one year older than mine at the same middle school. He was a good eighth-grade kid. His skin still had that little-boy look, but his mussed-up hair gave him an "I'm-almost-a-teenager" sass. Active in church. Doing well in school. Smiley and sweet. His mother was the quintessential stay-at-home mom in every aspect but one: Her hair was always flawless and nearly always a new color and style. Except for her hair, I would say that she was ultraconservative, with a desire to shield her son from the world—perhaps too much. But something had slipped past her vigilance.

"My son is dating an absolute *whore*." She burst into tears as soon as she said it. I was a bit stunned. Both the word and the fact that this sheltered kid was allowed to date in eighth grade were surprising. "He has no idea what he's risking. None! And we can't get him to stop."

She went on to tell me the name of the slightly older girl, the fact that she was in high school and was already "experienced." (Apparently that meant she'd had a lot of boyfriends and a lot of first kisses.) In my friend's opinion, the *girl* had pursued the relationship. Her son was the innocent younger man blindsided and mesmerized by the attention.

"What should I do?" she asked. At this point, I began to ask the Lord for wisdom. I didn't know enough to get this answer right, but I couldn't afford to get it wrong. I waited a moment as she pulled out some tissues and blew her nose. And then the answer seemed to come from heaven.

"When did you take time to communicate to him what your family dating standards are?" I asked.

"We haven't done that yet," she said. "He's not ready."

Apparently, he was.

That's why we're writing this book.

So you'll be ready. And so your son will be.

Most parents don't realize just how high the stakes are or just how soon they become a factor. When we do our seminar on raising sexually pure kids, Bob always says, "I know that it seems impossible that the sweet, innocent kid sitting across the dinner table from you could possibly be having the same kinds of thoughts and feelings you had when you were exactly his age, but *he is*. I promise you, *he is*."

We want to think that our son won't notice the Victoria's Secret poster or the Hooters billboard, but he will. We hope he won't fall prey to the aggressive girl that flirts with a promise of something more, but he could. And we really pray he won't be overcome by hormones, becoming the kind of guy that preys upon others to satisfy his sexual urges. But those are very real physical desires. Left undirected, he won't know what to do with them except what instinct tells him to do. And that's why we have to prepare him *before those things become a factor*. (If reading this makes you want to put this book down because your son is "only eight," don't be too quick. This book is for you. Let me prove it in this chapter.)

The fact is, our "good" sons have only a 50/50 chance, statistically speaking, of making it through high school without experiencing one of the following: sexual sin (and that's without the even higher risk of porn use), succumbing to an emasculated version of manhood resulting in a loss of purpose and leadership, and experiencing significant depression.

Bob and I counsel parents every day who "did everything right" and can't understand how their son could be the one dropping out of high school, dating the wrong girl, or addicted to gaming and porn. You can do a lot of things well but innocently skip critical conversations and activities that build moral values in your child. The foundation for the development of a good man of honor and integrity is actually built when he is a boy between the ages of 8 and 12, when he is a tween.

The mother–son connection

Your relationship with your son matters. A study of 265 mother–son pairs, following from the boy's fifth year to adolescence, found that boys who had close relationships with their mothers had healthier teen years and close relationships with risk-averse peers. Conversely, those with disconnected mother-son relationships were more at risk of delinquent activities during the teen years.[1] Want your son to be a good guy as a teen? Invest in the currency of time to build a strong bond now.

What Are the Risks?

Before I wrote this book, I asked my good friend Kelly to do three months of research on the greatest pitfalls facing your son in our culture. Then we asked moms on our ministry website what their fears were. Not surprisingly, these pitfalls and fears matched up. Moms intuitively know what to be concerned about. The most predominant risks seem to be these four.

1. Our sons are at risk of being emasculated and robbed of their desire to be good by our feminist culture. This is *our* greatest concern about boys today. As Bob and I shared in the last chapter, we believe that the feminist movement made saviors of our women and villains of our men.

(We're very grateful that women can vote, are competitive in the salary pool, and have become more educated...but maybe we have gone too far. Do men have to be classified as "bad" in order to allow women to reach their fullest potential?)

Exposure to a message like that will eventually lead to you believe it, and men *in general* have chosen to live according to this lie. Specifically this shows up in the way they approach education and career goals. (One mom we interviewed has a son who's a good eighth-grade boy in every way. But she's frightened by his complacent acceptance of B's in school when she knows he's capable of so much more if he just cared!)

Boys are twice as likely to drop out of high school. And, for every 100 girls expelled from public elementary and secondary schools, 335 boys are.[2] This trend of failing to perform academically continues into a young man's twenties.

State University of New York professor Michael Kimmel notes that

> the traditional markers of manhood—leaving a home, getting an education, finding a partner, starting work and becoming a father—have moved downfield as the passage from adolescence to adulthood has evolved from "a transitional moment to a whole new stage of life." In 1960, almost 70 percent of men had reached these milestones by age of 30. Today, less than a third of males that same age can say the same.[3]

Since we believe that men were created to be leaders of their families and diligent providers, this is a tragic mark on the very definition of manhood as designed by God.

What takes up the time that boys and young men formerly devoted to being male leaders striving to succeed in education, career, and building a family? Trouble, in the form of our other three big concerns for boys. In fact, says Michael Gurian, "The fear we need to have for these young boys is that they will move further into trouble and further away from success."[4]

2. Our sons are at risk of falling prey to our highly sexualized culture. As I listened to you in preparation for writing this book, the sexualized culture is *your* greatest concern for boys today. When I asked what you were afraid of, many of you wrote things like this:

> *"Pornography…by far the biggest battle!"*
>
> *"Porn enslaving his mind."*
>
> *"The sexual publicity…billboards, commercials, stores in the mall…"*
>
> *"Pornography and sexual sin…"*
>
> *"Sexual visual stimulus EVERYWHERE."*
>
> *"Easy access to porn."*
>
> *"That he will pick the 'wrong' kind of girl."*
>
> *"Respecting the girls. Even when they aren't respectable."*
>
> *"Aggressive girls!"*
>
> *"Girls are far too aggressive today."*
>
> *"Aggressive girls with an agenda!"*
>
> *"I want to teach my son to stay pure and I don't want anyone to give him grief about it."*
>
> *"Boys are almost expected to sleep with as many girls as they can or else they will lose their 'man card.'"*
>
> *"Falling prey to peer pressure when it comes to intimate relations."*
>
> *"Giving in to sex to get popular."*

Porn, aggressive girls, and outright sex. Triple threat.

Even tween boys are being treated for porn addiction these days. In one survey, 42 percent of Internet users ages 10 to 15 said they'd used porn online recently.[5] We believe it's significantly higher than that. Why is the problem bigger than it used to be decades ago? Our grandfathers didn't have to drive by Hooters billboards. We live in a pornographic culture.

Aggressive girls are initiating sexual relationships. Girls weren't just told they had to have jobs, they were told they had to have the same drives and sexual instincts as men. Just about the time the feminist movement told women to burn their bras, Gloria Steinem said that "a liberated woman is one who has sex before marriage and a job after." (Thanks, Gloria. That one has served our sons well, not to mention our daughters!)

Click here!

Go to familylife.com and search for "The Link Between Sex and Attachment." You'll discover three of the most groundbreaking audio programs on teens and sexuality that exist. Drs. Joe McIlhaney and Freda Bush explain the chemicals of sexuality (including dopamine, which is a chemical you'll learn a lot about in this book!).

Roughly half of all boys will leave high school having been fully sexually active. And while there seems to be a recent small shift toward more students choosing abstinence, if they decide to be sexually active the news is really bad. The average number of sex partners rises each year as hooking up and "friends with benefits" makes casual sex more and more acceptable.

While we arm our boys to be ready for those aggressive girls, we need to teach them to stand up and man up to win the battle with porn and sex. A special mention goes to Hugh Hefner for co-opting the term *playboy* for his porn magazine. "Think of the refusal of adult manhood implied by the title alone!"[6] Which brings us to the next area of attack on our young men.

3. Our sons are at risk of losing their sense of responsibility in the real world as they find a false sense of purpose in the male gaming culture. Boys— abetted by many of their parents as they pull out credit cards to endorse the addictions—are "winning epic battles" in a virtual world. Nielsen reports that the average family spends more on gaming than on printed literature, premium TV, home video, or music.[7] Gaming is a $48.9 billion industry globally. And, we admit, our family has fallen prey to it.

Many researchers have warned of the addictive and neurochemical impact of gaming. There is a very real physical reaction occurring during all that fantasy world fallout. As the authors of *PlayStation Nation*,

Olivia and Kurt Bruner, have noted, the chemical reaction that results in the body is so powerful that children in the hospital who were gaming needed less pain medication than those who simply watched TV as a distraction. The Bruners likened the phenomenon to an amphetamine drug injection. Very powerful!

The most startling piece of research we discovered as we studied boys and gaming was unearthed by author Michael Gurian. Gurian correlated addiction to gaming with a decline in a boy's pursuit of life purpose. He proposed that a boy with too much screen time can gain a false sense of purpose. His research into the male brain revealed that when a boy "wins" on-screen he gets a jolt in his brain—"like a hit of cocaine." This jolt feels like success to him. It makes his male-craving-a-life-mission brain feel like it's accomplished something. It hasn't. In the real world he's accomplished almost nothing.[8]

The mental-emotional results of this false sense of purpose, coupled with the addiction to all things sexual, often leads to our final concern for today's boys.

4. Our sons are at risk of drowning in depression. Eighty percent of stimulant medications prescribed are for American *boys*.[9] Boys are five times more likely to commit suicide than girls.[10] Alcohol use, the number-one youth problem in America,[11] is more likely to lead to depression in boys than it is in girls.[12]

Depression for boys is often masked by anger as they seek to be "strong." And while there are many contributing factors to the anger in today's tween and teen boys, there is one that's more important than all the rest: the absence of a father in their lives. I know that about half of the moms who read this book don't have the privilege of sharing the task of parenting with an engaged dad. For that, I am deeply sad. (See our "Singled Moms" sidebar on the next page for a quick dose of courage right now if that's you.) A father is a crucial role model and mentor for a boy, and his absence can contribute greatly to the risk of depression.

And this is where the cycle becomes vicious for our sons. A depressed individual is less likely to make good moral decisions and often seeks to "self-medicate" the emotion. Porn, attention from a willing girl, and falling into the fantasy world of gaming are all proven to be forms of emotional medication for depression.

Clearly a mom has a lot to be afraid of for her son in this overtly sexualized, emasculated culture, where few are rising up to encourage and help boys to become good men. Perhaps the most concise description of this fear came from a mom who wrote, "I fear that all we do to teach him responsibility to God and others will not be enough to balance out the 'me' attitude and general irresponsibility of the world."

Singled moms

While neither Angela Thomas nor I would shy away from stating the firm truth that a home with both a mother and father is optimal for any child, I want to stay away from making you feel like raising a good son isn't possible without a dad. In the "Singled Moms" sidebars I asked Angela some of the tough questions…

Is it possible to rise above the stats?

"Yes! Do you know why? Because of the Lord! Where the Spirit of the Lord is, there is truth. There is wisdom. There is healing. People tried to hand me books about the statistics on how divorced kids grow up. But where the Lord is, there is freedom. If a mom is begging for the fullness of the Spirit over her home, she is a redeemed woman who is healed. You can take your statistics and go! We're going to put our boys on the altar of the Lord God Almighty. I'm gonna drag their bottoms to church…I'm going to do everything I can do to help the Lord make them into what he's purposed."

—Angela Thomas, author of *My Single Mom Life*

It's Time to Defend the Good in Our Boys!

God created men to be a picture of Christ's self-sacrificing love. Which means a man must be willing to lay down his own life and desire to protect and provide for a wife and children. I believe that men should be the primary (if not sole) parent bringing in income for a family that he leads lovingly with a selfless heart. (In some homes the income equation may be reversed, but the attitude of male leadership can still be observed.) The portrayal of Christ in these relationships is the greatest reason for us to cultivate the good in our sons.

The more inky the darkness, the more vivid the candle. You get the privilege of guiding your son to become a leader (rather than a slacker); a man who honors and values women (not a playboy); a purpose-driven man (not one lost in unreality); and ultimately, a man who is unselfish and willing to sacrifice his own comforts for the sake of his family and his neighbors. Just think of the impact he will have! Let me urge you to focus more on God's promises than the world's threats.

I had an amazing encounter with the Lord the day I began to write this book. My dear Robby, at the time nearly 21, was facing some big decisions that tested his goodness. And this mom had her face buried in the fibers of the carpet in intercession. It was the last day of the month, and that meant I would be reading Proverbs 31. Do you know that for the first time I realized that this proverb, which is most often used to instruct women, was written to *a son*! Further, although it was written by a king, it was taught to the son *by his mother*! (Not kidding. Read the first verse.) It could have been written for us today.

Would you indulge me for a moment as I introduce you to the DGV, Dannah Gresh Version, of the Bible? Verses 2-7 of Proverbs 31 basically say this:

> *Watch out for aggressive girls!*
>
> *Avoid rebellious friends!*
>
> *Men of honor don't get drunk, so leave the beer for those so far gone that it's their only hope to overcome depression!*
>
> *You should spend your time thinking not about yourself, but about the needs of others—those who can't speak up for themselves, the poor and needy.*

That doesn't sound like a guy who's been caught up in the "me" culture of the Old Testament (not much has changed, huh?), but rather one who is "good"—useful! What's a useful guy get as his reward? A girl!

You see, the rest of the chapter breaks into what is still the prayer of a mother's heart today. If I could boil down the next 21 verses into one promise from God for your son it would be,

God has a better-than-rubies girl waiting just for you!

And we're pretty sure the *only* thing she's aggressive about is having a heart for God and family.

Not every single one of our sons will be married. (And the apostle Paul said that was good in its own way.) But most will be married, because it is in marriage we're the fullest picture of God's communal character and Christ's self-sacrificing love. Let's stop acting (and talking) like it's not absolutely 100 percent cool to want our kids to aspire to the wonderful experience of marriage and family!

In this book, I hope to encourage you in cultivating a heart of good in your boy so he can be a man of integrity, honor, and purity...in contrast to the selfish, emasculated, irresponsible men our culture is churning out. My first goal: to help you become a "connecting mom." You may already be one—especially if you read *Six Ways to Keep the "Little" in Your Girl*. While some of the material in the next few chapters will sound familiar, you don't want to miss what is new and unique to boys. I just about had a heart attack researching the male brain and how it approaches connecting. (Have I mentioned *testosterone* yet? Yikes. Buckle up!)

"If I could change anything,
I would not work part-time. I asked
my son Eric when he graduated
from college if there was anything
he wished was different growing up,
and he said he wished
I had not worked part-time."

Janet, mother of grown sons
Tim, Chris, and Eric

CHAPTER 3

Becoming a Connecting Mom

———

I can't do it," pouted my dejected then-fourth-grade son.

"Can't do what?" I asked as I plopped some chocolate-chip cookies and milk in front of him on our kitchen table. They were his favorite. From day one, he thought that chocolate-chip cookies were one of two major food groups. (The other is wings.)

"My homework!" he said, and his lip started to quiver.

"Tell me about it," I said. And my normally strong, introverted boy spilled his stressed-out guts to me.

"You know what this is," I said matter-of-factly when he'd completed his lament. He looked at me, amazed that I had a diagnosis for the ills that troubled him. "It's your first case of grown-up stress."

"Stress?" he asked, and straightened up with a bit of pride that this was a "grown-up" ailment.

"Yes, and I can tell you how to fix it." It was on that day that I shared with my overachiever the secret that you don't have to do every single assignment above and beyond the call of duty. I take credit for the fact that, to this day, he reads a description of an assignment, meets the requirements, and then wraps things up. Incidentally, this secret hasn't hurt him, as he has managed to both keep stress down and do very well in school over the years.

Except for one adventuresome and delightful year, I haven't been a homeschooler. (That one year was a well-thought-out decision to separate one of our girls from the chaos of peer pressure and to remind her that we—Mom and Dad—are the ones who "know stuff" and who she should turn to for advice.) Thus, some of the sweetest memories I have in connecting with my children as tweens occurred when they arrived home from school. I loved getting my heart at peace and focusing on greeting them in a special way as much as I was able. Still do. (Last week Autumn and Lexi came home to a strawberry shortcake surprise. The fact that they were high-school girls did not deter them from squealing with delight!) As I think over the wonderful years of raising my kids, some of my most critical moments of parent–child connection happened just as that yellow school bus pulled away from our drive!

Parent–child connectedness can be defined as "being closely bonded by common traditions and frequently occurring activities." I think a good short definition would be "intentional togetherness." It's eating dinner five or more times a week as a family as opposed to eating on the run or in front of the television—or other screens. It's dusting off the *Christmas Comedy Classics*

The dad connection
by Bob

Dannah truly is wonderful at this connecting thing. It is so much harder for me to have those eyeball-to-eyeball conversations. A lot of times the drive home from school sounded like this:

Me: *"Robby, how was your day?"*

Robby: *"Good."*

Me: *"Oh, good."*

But the fact that I was driving him home from school was a form of connecting. Don't focus on your weaknesses in connecting. Focus on your strengths.

CD to play "Grandma Got Run Over by a Reindeer" and "The Hat I Got for Christmas Is Too Big" to officially ring in the holiday season. (Maybe your family traditions are classier than ours?) It's getting excited about laser tag in all its glory when your son is ten, and hosting a 9.3 hour Lord of the Rings trilogy marathon when he's fifteen. It's playing with, camping with, cooking with, and studying with your child. Quality time? A myth! Our kids need quantity that comes with great quality here and there.

> "Creating a connected child is the most important task in child rearing." [1]
> —*Edward M. Hallowell,*
> *author of*
> Driven to Distraction

Through the years the Gresh parent–child connectedness efforts have changed and adapted, with a few exceptions: We are diehard about eating meals together often and going to church. But when our kids were smaller, we connected through simple things like lazing around in our backyard pool at our Rolla, Missouri, home and taking "float" trips down the Meramec River. (That's "canoeing" for those of you who haven't spent any time in the Ozarks.)

Recently, a lot has changed…even since I wrote *Six Ways to Keep the "Little" in Your Girl*. Not only are our children older teens and young adults, but we have bought a farm. Connecting now often occurs as we chase down the most recent runaway, be it a peacock or a horse. (It's *Green Acres* all over again!) We love sleeping in on Sundays—our church meets in the evenings—and it's my honor to wake the family to big country breakfasts. And our very own eggs collected through the week are usually center stage. (The recipe at the end of this chapter is a favorite I make often.) Big family game nights that we all enjoy with the Stauffers, Browns, or other families are a *must* to sprinkle into our busy schedules.

Your family's traditions may be a lot different. It doesn't matter *what* connects you. It just matters that you create intentional togetherness—and a lot of it.

Singled moms

How did you handle traditions?

"During the first year of my marriage separation, I didn't decorate for Christmas. My son's teacher called and said, 'I know you're hurting, and I'm hurting for you, but Grayson was sad that you didn't decorate for Christmas like you've always done. No matter how much you're hurting you've got to do this for your children.'

"From that conversation forward, I didn't miss a thing. My children loved for me to put up dinky little things for every holiday. Easter baskets. A Valentine's Day candle.

"Traditions are very soothing and security-giving. We played the card game Uno a lot on my bed. Even the three-year-old could play Uno. I'd say, 'Just one hand tonight!' Then we'd play four or five. There was something about playing together that made it feel like everything was going to be okay. Your three-year-old sister just killed you in Uno, but things are going to be okay!"

—Angela Thomas

The Connection IQ Quiz

Let me give you a little tool in the form of a quiz. It'll help you to take a quick assessment of how well you're connecting.

	Often	Some-times	Hardly ever
I can name my son's three best friends.	3	2	1
I praise my son for diligence in school.	3	2	1
I don't know his friends' moms.	1	2	3
I talk about his inner strengths (such as integrity, honor, purity) as opposed to his external strengths (such as his physical strength, success in school, or handsomeness).	3	2	1
When I converse with him, he does a lot of the talking. I listen.	3	2	1

	Often	Some-times	Hardly ever
I tell him stories about my childhood.	3	2	1
I tell him stories about his dad's or grandpa's childhood.	3	2	1
I know what his favorite food is.	3	2	1
He watches most of his television shows without supervision.	1	2	3
My son loves reading OR our family has a reading goal/program that encourages it.	3	2	1
I make dinner for my family.	3	2	1
I (or his dad) am/is physically active with him.	3	2	1
I have talked to him, or I'm planning to talk to him about his body changes. (You get credit if dad is on this!)	3	2	1
He has a girlfriend.	1	2	3
We watch television together (as opposed to alone).	3	2	1
He is on the computer/Internet unsupervised.	1	2	3
I'm not able to help with carpooling for extracurricular activities.	1	2	3
My son's play time is made up of interactive adventure games (such as cops and robbers, paintball, board games, and so on).	3	2	1
My son has a "tribe" of men that includes a father figure, other godly role models, and peers who share our family values in their homes.	3	2	1
I talk to him about money management.	3	2	1
I know who his favorite teacher is.	3	2	1
The family computer has a safety filter.	3	2	1
I spend at least half an hour a week with him doing something special. (You get credit if dad does this.)	3	2	1

	Often	Some-times	Hardly ever
I know who his real life mentor/role model is, and I help them spend time together.	3	2	1
My child has chores to do.	3	2	1
We talk about girls.	3	2	1
My son spends a lot of time alone and doesn't have a male role model OR he spends most of his time with friends who are not good influences.	1	2	3
The family computer is in a public place so my son's Internet viewing is monitored naturally.	3	2	1
I know his favorite singer.	3	2	1
I know his favorite television show.	3	2	1
I am actively involved in carpooling for his extracurricular activities.	3	2	1
My son plays mostly electronic games (such as PlayStation, Internet games, etc.).	1	2	3
I have begun to expect my son to treat me (and any sisters in the home) as a gentleman would treat a lady.	3	2	1
I talk to his friend's moms about parenting our sons.	3	2	1

Total points: _____

Now that you've taken the Connection IQ Quiz, let's find out how you did.

Validation: Scored over 70

Congratulations! If you scored over 70 on this Connection IQ Quiz, it's because you're already intuitively connecting with your son in the areas most critical to value formation in boys aged 8 through 12. Let this book affirm what you're already up to by reinforcing *why* you are making these choices, so you can communicate effectively to other moms and get them in our plan. It will encourage you to stay the course.

Becoming a Connecting Mom

Clarification: Scored between 35 and 70

Hanging in there! This book is going to be a great tool for you! You're doing really well at forming your son's value system in some areas, but you need a little bit of clarification because you're missing key conversations in other areas. As you learn the "Six Ways" to form his value system, try to identify the ones where you scored lower by coming back to this quiz and reviewing it. This way, you'll know where to give special attention.

Resuscitation: Scored under 35

Oops! If you find yourself falling short in most of the Connection IQ Quiz categories, this book is going to be the means of breathing life back into a needy mother–son relationship. Don't feel bad. There are a lot of reasons why you might score this way, including stress in your own life, a recent family loss or divorce, or simply not having a good role model in your own mother. You're not a bad mom, or you wouldn't have this book in your hand! And you can raise a good boy. You just need to be more intentional in how you parent in order to successfully form your son's value system. I'm here to help with that!

No matter how you scored on the Connection IQ Quiz, welcome to the world of being a connecting mom. It's official. From this day forward, you are one.

Potato-crusted meat-and-potato "keesh"

Cooking! A fantastic way to foster the mom–son relationship. My philosophy on food is that when Dad is in charge, they can eat pizza and frozen pot pies. When I'm around, they get healthy food and the message to take care of their bodies.

Breakfast is no exception, but I couldn't put my fingers on what my young adult Robby really loved when he was living at home. So I texted him and asked why his "connecting mom," who knew what snacks, desserts, and dinners he loved, couldn't identify his favorite breakfast food. Our conversation was priceless.

Random Bob Thought: Not totally fair—we also order Chinese food when I'm low on gas.

> Robby: *"I don't eat breakfast, but I like keesh [sic] and coffee cake."*

> Me: *"Is this my 3.67 GPA, thin-film-coating-intern of a son? It's 'quiche.' And that'll come back to haunt you."*

> Robby: *"Hoocked on foniks werkd 4 me."*

So, here's my recipe for "keesh."

    2 cups frozen shredded potatoes
    1 tablespoon vegetable oil
    4 eggs
    1 can evaporated milk
    ½ cup thinly sliced baked ham, chopped into pieces
    ¼ cup diced onions
    1 cup shredded cheddar cheese
    salt and pepper to taste
    parsley flakes

Preheat oven to 425 degrees. Mix potatoes and oil in glass pie pan. Cook for 15 minutes or until potatoes are lightly browned. While cooking, whisk eggs and milk. Add salt and pepper to taste. Remove potatoes from oven and layer onions, ham, and cheese into pie plate. Pour liquid mixture over it and sprinkle with parsley. Bake for another 30 minutes or until firm to touch.

"As my boys grow and mature I am often moved to tears to think about my sons growing apart from me. As a female, I pray daily that their maturity and puberty experience won't make things 'weird' between us. I am realizing how quickly these little-kid days go, and I am cherishing every day!"

Nicole, mom of Braden, 8, and Grayson, 6

CHAPTER 4

Why Connecting Matters

I am getting better at this mom thing. It's taken me only 21 years to figure my kids out, but I just put together 24 hours of spot-on parental connection. Can a mom who has blown it more times than she can admit take a moment just to revel in a good day with you?

It all started yesterday with Lexi. She's having some drama right now... and not the kind that landed her the role of Audrey in *Little Shop of Horrors*. She's my extroverted, talking processor. It was no surprise that after a challenging conversation with a friend she marched right into my bedroom and plopped onto my bed. She stayed there for one hour. Close, connected, touching, talking. I just listened. (One thing I've learned about teenage girls is to just shut up and listen when the drama is on overdrive!)

Random Bob Thought: Where am I when this touchy-feely stuff happens?

Then there was the sudden appearance of Robby, my now

21-year-old son, who announced he was spending the night under the guise of needing to have his laundry done. He stayed well into the next morning, much to my delight. He's my introverted, thinking processor. He sat at the kitchen table working on math that would give Einstein a headache while I was in the living room working on this book. We didn't talk much, touch, or even *seem* to connect. Oh, but we did. And, for one of the first times in connecting to him, I realized it *was* actually connecting! Eureka!

And finally, there is Autumn. She's my 17-year-old who I've had for only three and a half years. She's my strong survivor. The Lord is doing such a good work of healing in her, and she wants to be close like Lexi, but she's stuck in a fallacious place of introversion sometimes because that's been safer her whole life long.

She was gloomy yesterday, but an afternoon session with our horse Trig allowed her to connect to me by connecting through him. Horses have a special ability to heal and help us connect, because they actually aid in the production of oxytocin, a bonding chemical that all of our brains crave and need to enjoy relationships! When I couldn't get Autumn to connect with me after she'd spent a good half hour feeling fearful as we tried new things in the saddle, I regrouped. Taking the saddle off so she could feel Trig's warm, wonderful body, I told her to climb on and just hug that 1000 pounds of palomino for 15 minutes until she felt safe.

Staying nearby on my own faithful four-footed friend, I soon saw Autumn's once rigid foot begin to comfortably sway back and forth. Before long, she opened up to me and we had a great talk.

Yep, it was a good day of mothering.

(Don't you wish they could all be like that?)

My kids are individuals. They each connect differently to me. A connecting mom has to know and understand each unique personality to be able to connect effectively.

In this chapter, I want to lay a foundation for you about why connecting matters and what the Bible says about it. This chapter is pure review for you if you've enjoyed *Six Ways to Keep the "Little" in Your Girl*, but it's much too critical to leave out if you haven't. So you have permission to skip ahead to chapter 6 if you have already heard this. Otherwise, settle in with a chai latte for some amazing illumination.

Why Does Connecting Matter?

Your son's brain development relies on connecting. This started when he was just a baby. In 2005, the findings of a new study released in *Pediatrics* found that parent–infant connection—intentional togetherness—plays a key role in shaping the right side of an infant's brain during the first year of life.

> *"We've been looking into the brain of an infant, knowing it will double or triple in the first year of life and found it is not just shaped by genetics but also by experience in the last trimester of pregnancy through the child's first year and a half of life," says Allan Schore, a leading neuroscientist at the University of California. "A parent or other caregiver can provide this early attachment, but large day-care situations may be less ideal."*[1]

Schore feels so strongly about the parent–child connectedness that should occur in the first year of life that he advocates a 56-week maternity leave, much like employees in Europe receive. This, he says, would positively impact the child's lifetime ability to handle stress and feel emotionally secure.

Furthering this important brain-development research is Dr. Joe S. McIlhaney Jr. of the Medical Institute for Sexual Health. His groundbreaking research on the brain proves that a second critical phase of brain development occurs just before and during puberty—at the older end of your boy's tweens. (For girls, this happens just a little earlier and begins just before puberty.)

"Research has shown that there are two periods in one's life during which there is explosive proliferation of connection between brain cells—during the last few weeks before birth and just before puberty," writes McIlhaney in his book on brain development and sexuality entitled *Hooked*.[2]

McIlhaney says that the part of the brain that remains to be developed after puberty is the prefrontal cortex of the brain's frontal lobes. It's located at the front of the head, behind the forehead. This area is responsible—among other things—to appropriate and control moral behavior or values!

He encourages me as a mom when he writes that "brains can be positively molded by structure, guidance, and discipline provided by caring parents and other adults."

These researchers are not just talking about the emotional and moral development of a child, but the actual *physical* brain growth. What they are really saying is that we ought to be connected—by physical proximity as well as emotional activity—so our children's brains can grow as God intended. It is more than just Mom and Dad being present to help navigate and influence decisions. There is an actual physical component involved. Your investment of time is helping your child procure the brain space to store moral values. And that gives you the ground to plant the values in.

> ### A call to cuddle
>
> It's been suggested that one reason boys may turn out "bad" is that they missed something special when they were infants. Parents talk to, cuddle, and breast-feed their baby boys significantly less than their baby girls.[3]
>
> The stereotype that a boy infant does not need as much affection is false. Since cuddling initiates the brain's ability to produce the chemicals of connection—oxytocin, serotonin, and more—failing to touch and be intimate with an infant does a lot of harm. With males, it may contribute to the "bad boy" factor by making them overall less intimate and able to connect emotionally, as well as putting them at more risk of violence and self-deprecation.

Your child is less likely to experience at-risk behaviors if he (or she) experiences parent–child connectedness. As I have continued my research from the late 1990s right up to the present, I have been bombarded by the words "parent–child connectedness." Connectedness reduces the risk of dropping out of school, crime, substance abuse, and sexual activity. It increases academic performance, social contribution, and the presence of healthy emotions and relationships.

Your child is more likely to experience positive, prosocial behavior if he (or she) experiences parent–child connectedness. This positive behavior might include academic, social, or spiritual success. It can also manifest itself as a sense of caring and concern in his family and friendships. In general, he'll be more socially responsible if he experiences...well, a little bit of family laser tag and a whole lot of dinners together!

What the Bible Says About Connectedness

A lot of people rightly point to a passage in Deuteronomy to affirm the concept of parent–child connectedness. Deuteronomy 11:18-19 reads,

> *Fix these words of mine in your hearts and minds; tie them*
> *as symbols on your hands and bind them on your foreheads.*
> *Teach them to your children, talking about them when you*
> *sit at home and when you walk along the road, when you*
> *lie down and when you get up.*

This is no doubt a passage encouraging you and me as moms to know God's value system as written in his Word and then to spend connecting time—sitting at home and walking in the way—impressing it into our children's hearts. It's probably the most direct biblical encouragement to connect as a means of teaching values.

But I'd like to direct you to a different passage as our core verse as we look at connection. It'd be a valuable one to memorize and take to heart, especially considering the deeper meaning I'm going to share with you. Proverbs 22:6 reads,

> *Train up a child in the way he should go, and when he is old*
> *he will not depart from it* (NKJV).

At first glance, it is easy to see that God is affirming "the way" that is right for us to follow in general. And that's correct, because the word "train" is the Hebrew word *hanak* and would be best translated "dedicate."

This indicates that our children are to be dedicated to God and his ways. But there is a deeper treasure hidden in this verse for us.

The Hebrew word for "way" in this verse is *derek*. Literally, it means *"my"* way" or "bent." It was a Hebrew marksman's term. Hunters and soldiers of that day and age did not receive a standard-issue bow and arrow with wires and buttons to adjust the bow to the man. Rather, each marksman went out and found his own piece of wood and crafted it carefully into a bow. Since each bow was made of a unique kind of wood whose strengths and levels of moisture varied, it was likely that it took hours and days to actually learn the unique "bent," or tendency, of the wood so that a marksman could be accurate with it. The word *derek* refers to the process of learning the wood.

What I think God is saying to you and to me is this: "I've got a specific way that I'd like you to dedicate your child to follow, but to be successful you've got to know the unique strengths and qualities of your child. And by the way, that'll take some *time*. So plan on investing it. Remember what I said about 'sitting in the house' and 'walking in the road.' It's going to take a lot of that."

What a task we have as parents.

Not only do we need to know and absorb God's moral value system, but we've got to be students of our children—learning each child's "bent"—so that we can impart God's values in creative ways that will impact each child according to his or her unique differences.

In a word, your boy is an individual with his own God-given personality.

But there's another factor that often baffles an estrogen-drenched mama. You guessed it. Sometimes the very fact that they are *boys* will leave us wondering what is going on inside those developing noggins.

Singled moms

How do you get it all done and stay connected?

"I love this quote from Jill Briscoe: 'There is an art to leaving some things undone so that the greater things can be done.' I tried to have my work wrapped up by the time it was time to get my kids from school. No more business calls. No more e-mailing. I wanted to be able to look at them in the eyes.

"Dinners became something I had never envisioned. They were simple. Boil a few ears of corn and bake a chicken, and there was dinner. If we simplified things a whole lot, I could be nice! 'Tonight is baked potato night. Tomorrow night we're having pancakes.' You see? Keep it simple.

"It's all about staying connected. I didn't want to be a frustrated mom with four children. I wanted to be nice. Keeping it simple and leaving some things undone kept me nice."

—Angela Thomas

"My biggest concern is that right now he's happy with B's in school and isn't interested in working too hard on anything, sports included. He'll try—to a certain point."

Kim, mother of Christian, 13

CHAPTER 5

How Connecting
Forms Values

W e'll soon delve into a study of the male brain, but let me first introduce you to the three different stages of moral development. These stages help us to better understand why connecting to your son is so critical to his value formation. I hope you enjoy this fascinating insight into what makes your son believe what he believes, as we put on our geek glasses to roll up our sleeves for some social science.

The Copycat Phase

Between the ages of 2 and 5, your son is developing a set of moral values through imitation. Your son will want to model everything you do... and particularly everything his father does. His brain is saying, *Daddy does it. I want to be like Dad because that feels good. I will do it too.* He is acting out a *consequential* moral behavior. So, he "drives his car to work" or "builds a house for mommy" or "talks kindly on the phone to a friend."

During this season of his life, he needs toys and opportunities that allow him to copy the behavior you model. Car keys. A toolbox. Lincoln Logs. Telephones. Anything that lets him pretend he is you is a toy that helps with positive moral growth. This is a crucial part of creating a value system in him, but it does not cement your values into him. It simply introduces them.

The Counseling Phase

Between the ages of 6 and 11, your child is developing a set of moral values by asking you *why* you believe what you believe and do what you do. It is an *interactive* phase of moral development, characterized by asking a lot of questions as your child considers more variables. In his brain he is asking, *Why does Daddy do that? I think I want to be like Dad, but does it really feel good? Maybe I will do it too, if Mom can tell me why Dad does it.* He is beginning to monitor his own conduct based on what he thinks. If it makes sense to him, he'll do it. So, he asks a lot of questions—mostly "why?" You get to be his counselor as he figures out everything he believes about life! During this season, he may still be asking *you* the questions but they may be about *Dad's* values. He will also start to ask Dad directly.

Your son needs play and interaction that lets him practice monitoring his own conduct. A soccer ball to get a game started in the neighborhood. A tree house to build and improve upon. Even a community drainage pipe to explore. (More about that one in part two!) Anything that lets him enact scenarios that require analytical thought helps him with moral development. During this season, he is truly deciding what he believes. For that reason, I believe it is the most critical of the three stages, because his character is beginning to be molded and fixed.

The Coaching Phase

Between the ages of 12 through his adult years, your son is living out a moral set of values he has developed through asking all of those "why?" questions. This is a phase that involves *reasoning* as he allows his values to begin to affect his behavior. You and his dad are pretty much observers. It's not like you're in the stands and don't get to tell him how to play the game of life—you're more like coaches on the sidelines.

In his maturing brain he is asking, *How do I want to do this? Is there something* I *believe that will help me decide? Maybe* I *will do it, if it fits into what* I *believe.* He will falter a lot. Remember how we looked at brain development in the last chapter? All those new connections made just before the age of 12 are now beginning to grow and be strengthened. This will continue until he is in his early twenties, when his prefrontal cortex will be fully developed and he's finally capable of complete moral self-regulation.

It's during this season that your son needs you to help him develop his community. He needs healthy relationships and responsibilities that help him practice good character and monitor his own conduct in a safe environment. During this phase, he has already started to consistently live out what he believes, but you can help him in evaluating and adjusting his already formed value system.

Let's review.

The Copycat Phase	The Counseling Phase	The Coaching Phase
Age 2 to 5	Age 6 to 11	Age 12 to adult
Consequential copying	Considering beliefs	Adjusting beliefs

How Does Connecting Form Values?

During the Copycat Phase, you're close enough for your son to imitate. During the Counseling Phase, you're close enough to be the end-all source of all knowledge to every "why?" During the Coaching Phase, you're close enough to be there for all the conversations as your teen or young adult hits a crisis in belief. (A note about the teen years: I spend less physical energy on my kids now that they are teens and young adults, but way more mental muscle. Our deep conversations are fewer and further apart, but when we have them they are so very critical. I can't miss them. I have to be accessible.)

Can you see by looking at this that the most critical phase to value formation is right here, during his tween years? This is when his values are formed, not when he is a teenager. If you've waited until he is 12 to tell him that porn is bad, you'll have missed the beauty of telling him that God created women to be beautiful, *honored* creations of God. If you wait until he's 13 to tell him about wet dreams and masturbation, you'll have missed the beauty of telling him *why* his body is good and worthy of treating with integrity. If you wait until he's 14 to discuss sexual relations, you'll have missed the critical importance of telling him *why* God created marriage to be a one man–one woman picture of his love for us.

It's not that you won't be able to *try* to form his values after he's 13. It's just that the world will have already issued a fairly strong answer to the "why's" if you haven't, and restructuring his mind-set about how to live is a lot more difficult than building it from the ground up.

It takes time to answer the question "why?" But parents who refuse to take the time to answer the question often end up on one of two ends of a spectrum—creating either a legalistic or an anything-goes environment. Children who grow up in a legalistic environment—never knowing *why* a rule is a rule—tend to not internalize the values of their parents, and when you aren't looking they'll live however they want. Children who grow up in an anything-goes environment—where parents are buddies—generally lack the discipline to live out values you introduce to them. You need to be a mom who sets rules and uses your relationship with your son to help him understand *why* the rules are what they are. And that happens between the ages of 8 and 12, when he's actually asking the question.

As I indicated, introducing critical subjects after the age of 12 is like kayaking upstream! The question is not "*Should* I talk to him about girls, and sex, and wet dreams, and other stuff that scares me silly?" The question is "*How* do I talk to him about girls, and sex, and wet dreams, and other stuff that scares me silly *without robbing him of his innocence*?"

Speaking of being scared silly. Let's take a look at one more piece of the tween-boy puzzle before we dive into the Six Ways to Keep the "Good" in Your Boy. Yes, I'm talking about testosterone. Let's jump into it in the next chapter.

"At my son's recent physical I was given the usual sheet of 'What to Expect During Early Adolescence.' 'Wet dreams' was listed, so I talked with my pediatrician regarding my lack of understanding and my concerns. The next thing you know, they tell me masturbation is a part of life. So, as a female, I worry that I may have too-strict rules that may cause him to feel like a failure in areas of sexuality."

Amanda, mother of Cody, 11

CHAPTER 6

Warning: Male Brain on Testosterone Straight Ahead

I was startled the first time it happened. A full-out body slam. My then-12-year-old son surely didn't know his strength, but why would he want to attempt to crush at least a few important bones in my body?

"It's a love slam," my husband later explained.

"A love slam!" I lamented. *What would it feel like if that body-bruising blow wasn't seasoned with love?* I wondered.

I was confused.

Boys are so unlike us. But that cannot be an excuse for a mother to step back and let Dad do the parenting. In fact, a boy will only get half of what he needs if you don't do your part. I'll explain what half of value formation is best facilitated by Mom, and what half is best facilitated by Dad, as we move through this chapter. (As usual, there will also be help for single moms, so don't be discouraged if you don't have an involved father around.)

So how does a guy's brain work? How do we know, looking through our female filter, when our son is expressing love or when he needs guidance and admonition? This chapter will help you to do your part effectively and with the least amount of…well, body slamming!

Buckle up, Mom!

Let's dive into the male brain.

Introducing Testosterone

During a boy's tween and early teen years, his hormones and brain chemicals will change just as dramatically as a girl's will, despite the fact that a girl's changes are more noticeable. Specifically, the deep limbic system of a boy's brain is in overdrive. It will begin to be flooded with dopamine (which brings a taste for risk) and testosterone (which moves a boy toward aggressiveness). At the same time, his brain is experiencing a *lack* of serotonin (which creates a sense of relaxation and peace) and is less emotional overall. Sounds like a recipe for a body slam, doesn't it?

And it is.

At the same time—remember this from the last chapter—the prefrontal cortex of his brain isn't fully developed yet. This area of the brain takes control of setting priorities, forming strategies, controlling impulses, and pursuing ideas. It's a "cognitive" thinking area, which also includes making moral decisions. This is your son's moral-value brake system. Sadly, it's still "waiting on parts" until he's in his mid-twenties. Until then, he's got his aggression and risk putting part of his brain on overdrive. The engine is revved, the wheels are turning, but the brakes are likely to cut out when needed! He's going to have a hard time consistently making good self-control and judgment decisions.

Consider the fact that car rental companies don't rent to someone under the age of 25 without special arrangements. The research indicates that the risk of damage is higher when their cars are driven by drivers without all the parts in place in their prefrontal cortexes.

Is the risk greater for boys to make bad judgment decisions? Yes! Why? Because girls have the benefit of serotonin. Serotonin creates a sense of peace and relaxation, allowing them to make decisions more carefully and deliberately. Boys, on the other hand, are doped up on "aggression" (testosterone) and "risk" (dopamine).

But there's a huge upside: The unique wiring of your son's brain poises him for *goodness*! He may one day take the risk to build a Fortune 500 company that funds good works all around the globe. It may be second nature for him to kick down the door of a brothel to rescue a little girl from traffickers in India (or Indianapolis, sadly). Maybe he'll fight for family values in Congress. He may defend his co-workers from a predatory boss. Perhaps he'll risk the comfort of wealth to be a missionary to a remote part of the world. Maybe he'll stand out as honest in a company where "everybody" cheats and cuts corners. Aggression and risk-taking, properly channeled, release potential in our sons to become not only *good*, but *great* men!

Random Bob Thought:
Full disclosure — This bugs me.
They can drive a Humvee in the war,
but not a compact car from Avis?

And this is where Mom and Dad become crucial—because there's something that your son's brain does not naturally do for him during these years that it does do for our daughters. It doesn't direct the prolific changes taking place in his brain to be used toward health, purpose, and character. While a girl's brain presses her toward "good" by virtue of her extra dose of serotonin, which allows her to process things more slowly and emotionally, a boy's brain requires external pressure to move it in that direction.

We believe that God created the institution of families to define the direction and purpose of all this male aggression and risk-taking…and that a mother and father each provide a significant and unique contribution to character development.

The Unique Father–Son Connection

A dad is always a vital part of your son's life, but as he reaches his mid-tweens the value-formation process makes having a male role model even more critical. That's why I, Bob, would like to ask you to gently nudge your husband or your son's father to read this book with you. (I have no problem asking him to man up. So hand this book over to him for just a moment and ask him to read the next few paragraphs.)

From the age of 11 until his early twenties, a young man is learning to direct his aggression and risk-taking toward "good." (Or being allowed to let them naturally lead him to "bad.") A fundamental component of this is what we'll call his "call of duty." It is the process of learning to direct his energies toward a fulfilling life mission. This significance and fulfillment is more important to the male brain than to the female one. Women can be fully satisfied by having healthy key relationships in their lives. But guys, in general, need a calling to conquer. Here are a few things that a dad can do to successfully teach and model "call of duty" to a son.

Random Bob Thought: Hey, Dad! Man up!

Be intentional about connecting. While a boy is developing his sense of a call of duty, it is vital that a dad try to connect with him emotionally. If your son is going to use his potential for good, he's going to have to connect to other men who have done just that. Let's start with Dad!

This didn't come naturally for me. Dannah can tell you that I'm known as "the ADD guy," and being consistent isn't my forte. (However, I am very consistent about being late for meetings and forgetting things…like turning the car off when I get to work!) For me to be intentional about connecting with Robby, I had to schedule it into my calendar as an unbreakable weekly event. For most of his tween years we had a standing Thursday-night date. We headed to a local sports bar and ordered a greasy platter of wings. (Dannah may have given Robby his love for chocolate-chip cookies by mixing up batch after batch, but I'm responsible for his addiction to wings.)

Now, here's where father–son connecting can become difficult for a mom to understand. I remember week after week coming home, only to have this conversation.

> Dannah: *"What'dya talk about?"*
>
> Me: *"Nothing."*
>
> Dannah: *"You were together for two hours. You had to talk about something. Is it that you don't want to tell me?"*
>
> Me: *"No. We didn't really talk about anything in particular."*
>
> Dannah: *"It's not possible to spend two hours together without talking."*
>
> Me: *"Yes. It is. We just did it."*

Eventually Dannah would let it go, only to pick it back up next week. She will be the first to admit that she was nagging. I, Bob, understood that she didn't mean it. She just didn't "get" us, and I secretly enjoyed the intrigue of being mysterious to her. I didn't take it personally. But, to all the wonder-moms who picked up this book hoping to manage their husband because he's not engaging enough: *Maybe he is.* And he might need an "attaboy" from his favorite girl once in a while.

Many times I felt defeated, mired in bad-daditude because of my lack of deep conversation with Robby. But I now know that it was important for my son to just simply have me set that time apart to focus on him. I honored him with time, and he noticed. He knew conceptually that dads are busy and have important things to do, so it was a mark of his significance that I gave him my time. It told him that I loved him a lot. And while it might not seem like it to the average verbose female, we were getting a lot done. Let me explain what I mean by introducing you to the second thing a dad does to teach his son how to be good.

Just be around a lot to show him what a good man looks like. That's the primary goal of connecting to your son: just hang out and *be.* In our skin-is-in, beer-brawling, self-motivated world, your son isn't going to see many examples of good men in the media, on his sports teams, or at school. He has to meet them in the flesh, and you're the best place to start.

Maybe you're the dad reading this and you're saying, "But I'm not that good!" Memories of when you gave in to the skin-is-in culture or got drunk or greedy come back to haunt you. I have to admit I have some moments of departing from God's goodness that really bug me. But I've decided to use them for fuel to help Robby be a good man, rather than an excuse to stay out of the game of raising him.

Maybe you're a mom reading this and you're saying, "But my son's dad isn't that skilled at connecting to our son!" *Maybe he is*. I, Dannah, have learned that we girls can be very critical when we don't understand how guys relate and function. (Take, for example, a dad hanging out at a sports bar eating wings with his son for two hours and just *being*. I wish I could take those weeks of nagging back and just say, "Honey, thanks for being a great dad!") Be careful not to impose your female relational skills onto a male relationship, which is supposed to yield entirely different results than the one you will enjoy with your son. Can we ask you to get a good, solid, truth-telling girlfriend to help you figure out if you're just being too hard on poor ol' dad?

While we want to encourage you that the best role model for a son is his dad, we have to acknowledge that maybe your son's dad is not a good man. Maybe he's left you and isn't willing to be involved. Maybe he's simply a workaholic who can't overcome his addiction to reaching the next rung on the ladder. Maybe you do have a problem. Well, there's some good news even in the following section, because the final thing a dad should do, a mom can do if she absolutely has to.

Introduce him to a community of good men. We believe that it takes more than one good man to override the bad examples your son will meet on his journey. And we believe that the way men overcome the temptation to be bad is by communal thinking and living.

One of my—Bob's—favorite authors is Nate Larkin. Nate founded an informal society for men because of the deep need in all of us to walk in community. He claims that the men of the Samson Society are "*real* men. Real *Christian* men. Real *screwed-up* Christian men. Separately we can act like complete morons, but together—together we are a formidable force for good, an alliance to be reckoned with."[1] Your son's community should be made up of Dad, other men your son can look up to as role models, and peers who choose to live well and have the parental support to do so.

Men crave this communal aspect of living, and if left to his own devices, it will be your son who chooses the people he hangs out with and emulates. That's not a good idea. We think it's much better for the father—or mother if absolutely necessary—to introduce him to a healthy community of good men.

This community of men doesn't have to be "official." In fact, it's better to think of it as encouraging relationships with good role models. You can't force it or create it. You have to pray for it and then support it when it happens.

Robby is quite different from me. Example: He is an engineer and is excited about going to conferences on corrosion. He talks about rust with the same kind of passion that I talk about marketing. To follow his passion he has to be focused, disciplined, and slow to make decisions—as opposed to my landscape view of life, which is marked by a quick pace and energy. Recognizing these differences requires me to connect him with other father figures or mentors who complement and add to his unique insight into life. They have been invaluable to help Robby.

When Robby was in middle school I, Bob, noticed a relationship kind

> ### Jethro
> ### (not the hillbilly)
>
> There's a beautiful biblical example of a man being fathered by someone other than his biological dad. The story begins in Exodus 2:18, when Moses is overwhelmed by his calling to lead Israel. Since Moses has no father to turn to, God sends in Jethro (not to be confused with Jethro from *The Beverly Hillbillies!*). If you need some extra encouragement that God has a godly father figure out there for your son, you might turn to Exodus and be inspired as you pray the Scripture over your son's life!

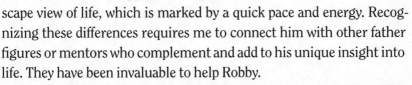

of clicking between him and his youth pastor, Don Jones. At this time our family was going through some challenges, so I simply asked Don to spend some time talking to Robby about it. It became a very strong mentoring relationship for him. There was no single man outside of our family that impacted him more thoroughly than Pastor Don.

A few years later, when Robby was in high school, I saw a connection occurring between him and his Christian principal, Pat Sullivan, and I simply encouraged it. Along the way, I've seen Robby pursue godly friendships with peers like Ryan Stauffer, Sean Devan, and Christian Horn. And I do whatever I can to connect to those young men too. My son's character depends, in part, on them. I want to know them.

It's not always the dad who creates these connections with other men. Angela Thomas had a unique way of accomplishing this as a single mom, and we'd like to share it with you. First, she was intentional about where she lived. She asked the Lord to open up an opportunity for her to live in a neighborhood where other families from her church also lived. God answered that request quite profoundly, prompting her to call her home "the blessing." (She writes about this in *My Single Mom Life*.)

Next, she identified three men in the neighborhood who were in great marriages and had thriving children. Then—notice this nearly imperceptible approach as opposed to demanding, asking, or pressuring them—she gave them permission to speak into her boys' lives. She simply said, "I want you to know you have permission to speak to my boys the way a dad ought to. If you see them out of line, you may speak into their lives. I pray all the time that they'll be caught quickly if they make a bad choice." (That prayer came in handy when one of the designated father figures found one of her boys trying to set a fire in the woods behind their home!) Today, those men are very proud of Angela's boys and feel like they've been very much a part of raising them.

Singled moms

How can you invite men into your son's life?

"I want you to know that you have permission to speak to my boys the way a dad ought to. If you see them out of line, you may speak into their lives."

—Angela Thomas

In a later chapter we'll talk about the concept of family love. A community of good men shows a boy how to direct his inborn call of duty to protect toward his family. But if a man isn't connected to his family—including both a mom and a dad—with a special kind of love, he doesn't have anyone to fight *for*. And then his aggressiveness and risk-taking can turn bad. Dannah and I hope that Robby grows up to have a lot of love for his wife and children. We are instilling a love for family into him by being connected to each other and our kids, and by encouraging him to connect with good men. We want to solidly anchor each of our children in the concept of family so they can build healthy ones someday. We believe that whether your original family is intact or you have become a blended or single-mom family, you will be able to help your boy learn to have family love.

The Unique Mother–Son Connection

While you are moving into the years when a dad's connection is so crucial, yours is still special. Your son bonds with you before anyone else on the planet, especially if you chose to breast-feed him. In most families, a mother is still the primary caregiver during the early years, and so your son has been raised primarily by you. Through your touch and voice, he has begun to learn the power of nurturing and being nurtured. This is a really critical part of his value-formation process. While some of the ways you touch him and nurture him will naturally begin to change with the explosion of testosterone just around the corner, you'll find that this change happens easily and you'll know intuitively what to change and when.

My giant of a young adult son is the cuddliest bear on the planet. He learned to be gentle and tactile from a mom who could barely keep her hands off him as a baby, carried him longer than she needed to, and always greeted him with a big bear hug as he grew. These expressions of nurturing are important to continue as your son moves into his tween years, so that he can be not only a strong father but also an affectionate one. (The occasional body slam may be his way of saying that he still wants to be tactile with you.)

The reward comes when you see him move out of those explosive years of testosterone called the tweens into a settling down of hormones where he can begin to return to a more gentle approach to living. One of my fondest memories of Robby's nurturing heart came when he and I were in Zambia during his senior year of high school. I turned around one day to see him lovingly holding a small orphaned boy. The little one had taken to Robby because the two of them had a similar scar on their arm. Through the barrier of two very different languages, touch became their conversation. My big, rough-and-tumble boy was sitting there nurturing this little child with touch. He had learned that from his mama!

Before Dannah starts to tear up and walk too far down memory lane, it's time to conclude part one of this little book. Hopefully you've gained a little bit of understanding in why connecting to your son matters, and how to do that. More practical tips are straight ahead in part two, as we explore the Six Ways to Keep the "Good" in Your Boy.

Part Two

Six Ways to Keep the "Good" in Your Boy

It's time to move from the philosophical to the practical. The second half of this book will introduce you to the Six Ways to Keep the "Good" in Your Boy. Each chapter will provide you with two tools that will help you apply general principles to your unique relationship with your son. They are...

God's Way

In each of the following chapters, you'll find a "*God's Way*" Bible verse. God's Word transcends time and culture and, as we will see, is applicable to parents in first-century Ephesus or twenty-first-century America. While you won't find a Bible verse that mentions PlayStation4 or the Internet, you will find verses that speak to those topics in surprisingly relevant ways. I'll point out one of these verses in the beginning of each chapter and apply it within the chapter.

His Way

Remember, Proverbs 22:6 encourages us to train a son to go *God's way* by being sensitive to *his way*, or bent. You know your son better than anyone else and are the perfect "author" to pen a plan for value formation in critical areas of his life. At the end of each chapter, you'll find a "*His Way*" assignment to map out your thoughts. This will include a prayer I have written based on the "*God's Way*" scripture and others I have used within the chapter. Be sure to end your time of penning practical ideas by praying this prayer out loud!

"The one thing we did right raising our boys was deciding to be teachers in the Virgin Islands. The boys were in their early elementary years. They got a chance to see what life is like outside of the U.S. and see how underprivileged kids live. It created a mind-set of thankfulness. They did not need *things* to be happy."

Nancy Martin, mother of adult sons Micah and Joel

CHAPTER 7

Way #1: Get Him Outside to Play

W hen Robby was in fourth grade we moved into a new development. His initiation by the neighborhood boys wasn't pretty.

I was still unpacking boxes, when I looked out the back of my house on a rainy day to see my somewhat indoorsy boy surrounded by a huddle of young manhood. There were three of them standing just outside a huge, mucky, dark, two-foot-wide drainage pipe. I could see that Robby was being "challenged" by a blonde boy, who I knew to be just one year older, named Ryan Stauffer. He seemed to want Robby to climb into that disgusting pipe!

What are they doing? I thought to myself.

I threw down my work and began to

God's Way

"Like a city whose walls are broken down is a man who lacks self-control."

PROVERBS 25:28

CORE VALUES: SELF-CONTROL, INTEGRITY

search for a pair of shoes to stomp right out there and tell those boys to behave. By the time I got out the front door I saw Robby laughing as he offered a hand down into a manhole, apparently at the opposite end of the drainage pipe, to lift an icky, mucky Ryan out of it. Robby, apparently, hadn't succumbed.

My neat, organized type-A personality thought Ryan's mom would surely be upset that his sneakers were wrecked and that she'd have to take a break from whatever she was doing to start a load of laundry.

But something in me nonetheless sensed that this was good.

And, in fact, this was very good.

Children are forgetting how to play.

Not the Stauffer kids. Tom and Jackie have raised three amazing kids—two young men and a girl—who know how to play. (When I later told Jackie about the drainage pipe incident, she just laughed and said, "Yeah, they do stuff like that sometimes!")

Random Bob Thought: I would have thought it was cool if he'd gotten into that pipe!

I consider Ryan—who, as I write this is one of Robby's roommates in his first apartment—to be one of the greatest positive peer influences in my son's life. And getting Robby to play outside was one of Ryan's best contributions.

At the time I didn't know just how critical a safety mechanism being outside was for a tween boy, but I know now. And, I see that the art of outside playtime is under attack by our culture.

In the 1950s—when the first episode of Disney's *Mickey Mouse Club* included an advertisement for Mattel's Thunder Burp Machine Gun—play began to be formed by what could be *sold*. In the 1980s, the Federal Communications Commission dealt a blow to healthy child play by taking away the restrictions on selling toys, clothes, and food directly to children through television. Since then, playing has become associated with toys. By that I mean we have a tendency to think our child needs a store-bought toy to play.

It wasn't always like that.

> Adam was created outside the Garden [of Eden],
> in the wilderness. Man was born in the outback,
> from the untamed part of creation. And ever since
> then boys have never been at home indoors, and
> men have had an insatiable longing to explore.
>
> —*Wild at Heart*, John Eldredge

Alan F. Lambert, a member of the Boy Scouts executive council, offered this as part of his congressional testimony on the risk boys are facing because of less access to unstructured outdoor play. He said,

> *Unstructured play [used to be] a significant part of our early childhood. Forts and tree houses were built in open spaces. Games—stickball, softball, dodge ball, football, capture the flag, kick the can, tag—you name it—were the order of the day. The games had no adult supervision and were put together by a group of kids playing. Members needed to be recruited, the rules were set and off we went.*
>
> *The healthy competition found in the games of my childhood are being replaced by the individual competitions found in the gaming world—PlayStations, Xboxes, etc. Play has become organized and structured—everything has a time and a place, a need for sign-ups, Mom's or Dad's help, and transportation.*
>
> *The result is a loss of imagination and the skyrocketing health issues associated with obesity and behavior [disorders.]*[1]

It wasn't always like that.

Old-fashioned play—consisting of forts and tag and the risk of an occasional broken bone—is good for our sons. It requires self-regulation, which is a skill necessary for becoming a healthy adult. Self-regulation is critical to the development and maintaining of moral values. So, how does a connecting mom get some good old-fashioned play into her son's life?

Get Him Outside

If your son, like mine, is happy to be behind a computer or a gaming system, this might sound like it won't work. I promise you, it can. And it must. Time spent building forts, climbing through drainage pipes, and building things with sticks, twigs, and rocks actually *helps* children to develop a crucial skill called *executive function*.

Executive function takes place in the prefrontal cortex, which, as I previously shared, is the part of the brain experiencing explosive growth during the tween years. It governs many different things for the human who possesses it, but one of them is to self-regulate—or to appropriate moral behavior and values. It's the ability that gives us the character quality of self-control.

Play and his self-control. The Bible says this about it: "Like a city whose walls are broken down, is a man who lacks self-control." Even though an ancient city's walls limited some of the freedom of its citizens, they welcomed them. Without walls, they were vulnerable to the attack of aggressors. So too, our sons are more vulnerable to attack—specifically, from things like porn—if they haven't built up the protective wall of self-control for their life.

The time to build that wall in your son is in his tween years, while the part of his brain that monitors self-control is experiencing explosive growth. Brain science aside, here's how experts theorize that the process of building executive function works.

If a boy spends time making up a new game to play in the street just outside his apartment building, he has to make decisions about the limits (rules of the game) and then choose to abide by them and hold his teammates accountable to do the same. Then, as his teammate *almost* scores one but misses, your son has to make a decision about his anger. Should he throw a rock at the kid his mind just dubbed a "loser"? His developing prefrontal cortex will hopefully help him to reason that "No! A teammate probably would *not* throw a rock at the kid just because he failed." Instead, he'll "self-regulate" by acting like a true teammate and learn to shout, "It's okay. Next time, buddy!"

This process of decision-making teaches your son self-control on many levels. (It might even help with ADD if he's struggling with it!) It's all about thinking through and choosing to follow behavioral norms, which does not occur when play is constrained by preset plans. As he learns self-control and how to regulate his behavior in the relatively safe outdoor play environment he will be better equipped to make responsible decisions when faced with the strong temptations the world will throw at him as he enters the teen years.

Random Bob Thought:
This is a paragraph obviously written by a mom. "It's okay! Next time, buddy!" was once, and only once, uttered by one of the early Church Fathers.

Not convinced just yet? There's another reason outdoor play is a must for any tween boy, and this is where I believe it becomes a mechanism to protect his integrity.

Play and his integrity. Let's talk about one of the greatest fears moms have for their sons in this culture. In correspondence via my Facebook page and websites, moms have made it clear that they're scared to death of porn.

And with good reason. Many of the adult men who've struggled with porn long-term and as an addiction say that the struggle began when they were a tween. With it came a complete breakdown of integrity because they lived in the bondage of a double life. Time and time again they report leading one life in front of family, friends, and church that was good on the surface, but another private life of evil and badness. The very definition of integrity demands a quality or state of being undivided, and a double-minded life is not that. Porn is, we believe, the tool Satan most commonly uses against young men today to strip them of integrity.

There's a very natural reason why men, as opposed to women, are so likely to fall prey to it. Leading research demonstrates that every time a boy or man looks at porn he gets a dopamine jolt. Remember—dopamine is that "risk-taking" chemical that is highly pleasurable and potentially addictive to testosterone-filled males.

Dopamine is not inherently "bad." Keep in mind that it's a strong force in helping your son pursue a life with passion and purpose and conquer the mountains he comes upon in his journey. However, dopamine is addictive— and it's one of the reasons it's so easy for tween and teen boys to fall victim to porn. Further, dopamine has a compounding effect: Once experienced, it creates a craving so strong a boy is willing to take greater and greater risks to experience it again.

While aiding our sons to build

How play lessens ADD

Many child-development experts are beginning to look at the lack of constructive play as a contributor to the rise in ADD/ADHD. Boys are at greater risk of ADHD and other neurodevelopmental disorders than girls are. Exactly why is not known, but some point to the fact that schools are taking away recess (due to liability and time-constraint issues),[2] parents are keeping their kids indoors (because of stranger danger), and kids simply desire to play outside less (their social world is only a keyboard away these days).

All of the chemicals a boy experiences in his tweens create a need for an aggressive, risk-taking outlet like recess! If he does not have this outlet, he is sure to experience frustration. On the other hand, studies of ADHD at the University of Illinois show that kids as young as five with those symptoms get much better with just a little bit of contact with nature.[3]

strong walls of self-control and sharing with them the dangers of porn and the rewards of God-designed marriage are helpful, they are effective only to a certain point. Boys, particularly in the tween, teen, and young-adult years, were created to live in a continual state of experiencing dopamine. They crave the craving, if that makes sense.

So what kinds of *healthy* risk-taking behavior can our tween boys participate in to satisfy their dopamine-craving and testosterone-filled bodies?

Here's the hopeful news for our sons. What if we took that same boy facing half-clothed women on every street corner, with porn only a click away on the Internet, and got him addicted to rock climbing, whitewater rafting, mountain climbing...or even just some serene rock-specimen-finding hiking for a boy less interested in adventure? Guide him into positive ways to tap into his risk-taking side—otherwise, lack of outdoor time plus increased computer time, combined with the churning chemical factory he shares with all our sons, creates an obvious point of risk for increased vulnerability to pornography.

Click here!

Go to amenclinics.com and click on the link labeled ADD/ADHD to see actual brain scans of patients struggling with the most common psychiatric disorder boys encounter. One look and you'll never doubt whether or not it is real!

I know that when you're staring at your ten-year-old three stories off the ground in a massive pine tree, the last thing you're thinking of is how he's taking healthy risks. But before going into mom-in-total-freak-out mode maybe you should pause and just let him be a boy on a big adventure in the great outdoors.

So, turn off the Xbox. Back away from the computer games. Take a break from too many guitar lessons and organized sports programs. Get a little outdoor playtime into your son's schedule! Be intentional about it, and protect it.

Give Him the Right Toys to Play with Inside

Of course, not every hour of every day will be spent outside. Creative play indoors is also critical to the development of your son's self-control. So what should he be playing with inside as a young boy and tween?

The best thing for him to play with is nothing at all. The "need" for toys has been created by multibillion-dollar corporate giants who really couldn't care less about the development of our sons. They care most about the unholy dollar. Our kids don't need anything to play *with*, and they play best when they are unlimited by toys that define play for them. They'll find the props they need—like a ripped blanket for a cape or mom's pot stick as a sword—as their imagination drives the playtime.

Of course, I'm not advocating that you have no toys whatsoever in your home. Connecting kids have toys. They just aren't consumed with them. So let's take a look at what kind of toys further the imagination—either inside or out—and allow for creative play.

The best toys boys can have during their tween years are the ones that aren't quite created yet. This means a pile of wood, some string, some matchsticks, and even paper are great tools to have handy. Of course, you have to know what to do with them to turn them into wooden toolboxes, clove-hitch knots, and the world's greatest paper airplane. (This is where a dad comes in really handy!)

Happy trails to city slickers!

Do you live in an apartment complex or high-rise with no green in sight? Don't let that be an excuse to let your son sit in front of the TV or computer all day. Schedule trips into the country. Join a city park play group. Find ways to get that boy outside! A Minneapolis/Saint Paul parents group took the "nature deficit disorder" diagnosed in their cities and started a class on "How to Play With Your Kids Outside." One of their primary sources for ideas is the Happy Trails Family Nature Club (HappyTrailsClub.net).

A book that my husband immediately gravitated toward when it first came out was *The Dangerous Book for Boys* by brothers Conn and Hal Iggulden. (Sadly, it was first published when Robby was nearly out of high school, but Bob enjoyed reading through it, and it became a gift for every new dad we knew for a few months.) How to play table football with a few quarters, how to create secret inks using anything from milk to lemon juice, how to build a tree house…I marveled at how the whimsical instruction opened my full-grown man's spirit to the wonder of boyhood. There's even advice on how to interact with the opposite sex: "Avoid being vulgar. Excitable bouts of wind-breaking will not endear you to a girl."[4]

I encourage you to pick up a copy of the book and wrap it up as a gift for your son's dad or father figure—even if he's not your husband. Be sure to include an old coffee tin with the book's "essential gear" for boyhood: a Swiss army knife, a compass, a handkerchief, a box of matches, a shooter (as in a marble), needle and thread, pencil and paper, a small flashlight, a magnifying glass, Band-Aids (a lot of them), and fishhooks.[5] Father and son will both be playing like boys in no time.

If you are going to buy actual brand-name toys, buy things that help your son build. Brands like Lego, Erector, or K'nex have created an empire of products that require your son to use problem-solving and critical-thinking skills. (It's kind of like building a fort.) Rokenbok was our son's building set of choice thanks to his grampy and grammy. The system is integrated so that you can build complex structures and then use the wireless remote controllers to bring everything to life! Hours and hours of thinking and building. Days and days of fun. Weeks and weeks of a terribly messy living room!

Prepare to Say "No"

Of course, you'll still have to suffer the clutter of "toys" on the shelves. Some of it is okay. Some of it is not. There are those products marketed directly at our sons that are outright bad—Grand Theft Auto or Dungeons and Dragons come to mind—but some of them simply lack the ability to build executive function, and that makes them much less useful in building a good boy. For example, I regret falling prey to all the "computer-like" systems that supposedly helped my children learn. (They'll spend plenty of time in front of a computer. They don't need a child-sized version of your laptop named after a cute animal.) These aren't really bad, but they just don't require our children to think and explore and create.

Your son won't just survive, he'll *thrive* without the toys "everyone else" has. Saying "no" is critical to great parenting. And believe it or not, I think our kids secretly appreciate it.

Shaunti Feldhahn and Lisa Rice wrote a book every parent should read: *For Parents Only: Getting Inside the Head of Your Kid*. Their real-life interviews with 1000 teens and tweens revealed that deep down a child of any age wants his parents to assert themselves as the authority in the relationship. Seventy-seven percent of respondents said they want parents who "set reasonable rules; ensure that I do my homework, care about who I hang out with and how healthy I am; and try to create family time and stay involved in my life."[6]

There's no better time to establish yourself as the authority than now. Or to keep it up, as the pleas get more difficult. Here are a few motivating factors as you build up the guts:

1. *Communicate what you believe with your wallet.* I'm not big on boycotts. I like to stay positive—but don't buy the junk. Retailers only stock what consumers buy, and we can influence that if we stick together.

2. *It's your job to teach values, not to stock toys.* If you choose private or public school education, it's okay to let someone else teach your child how to read, write, or dissect frogs. But it's your job to teach right and wrong. Anytime a toy trumps value training, you've stopped doing your job. Let the lessons begin.

3. *If the answer is "no," show him he's not alone.* He's going to feel alone about a lot of things. It's just the life of being a tween. But use your convictions about a toy or activity to show your son that he has friends who are in the same boat. Robby was not a child who often pressed us to buy him a lot, and when he did ask for something it was rarely

inappropriate. However, we were always happy to bring the parenting of Jackie and Tom Stauffer into the picture to remind him that Ryan was enduring the same drudgery that he was! And he seemed to be turning out just fine…drainage pipes and all!

Keep Him Playing Creatively As Long As You Can

You may have an older son and be wondering about play in his life. Though it will be more challenging, try to engage him in play for as long as you possibly can. His prefrontal cortex is still growing until his early twenties, so creative play is important until then, and can continue to build his ability to be self-controlled. How do you get a teenager to play? Well, you might try enrolling him in a drama class. Maybe creative writing is an elective in his high school. Even things as simple as corny youth-group games can be helpful in role-playing and developing boundaries.

Here's something really cool that our editor noted: Men really don't ever stop playing. (And he's a guy, so he can say that.) Ideally a boy's play becomes hands-on-project types of playing, such as building his first rocking chair or helping Dad fix a car. So maybe the best way to keep him playing is to help him begin to collect the tools he'll need for a workbench when he's a young adult. My mom and dad started buying a tool each year at Christmastime for my brother when he was in middle school. In this way, they were helping him make a transition from childlike boy play to play for grown-up men.

And here's where it gets really "good." (And I mean that in the literal sense of how God means goodness to be useful!) All that hands-on project stuff becomes the skills needed to be useful, helpful and…well, good…for his community! It's your job to help him make that transition.

Be creative!

You know your son!

You can do this!

His Way

What thoughts came to mind as you were reading this chapter? Did you feel affirmed in how you're guiding your son to play, or did you feel convicted to make some changes? No one knows your son better than you. Take a few moments to write a plan of action to build a lot of the right kind of playtime into your son's schedule. Does it require canceling some of his organized sports or music lessons? Does it require you to be home more often, or to drive out into the country once a week for some fresh air and dirt to play in? Be willing to modify things as God's Spirit—not the words I write—leads you.

_____

_____

_____

_____

_____

_____

_____

_____

_____

_____

_____

_____

_____

_____

Prayer for self-control based on Proverbs 25:28

Dear Lord, I deeply desire to help my son build a wall of self-control around his life. I do not want him to be like a city whose walls are broken down. It is my desire that this wall would enable him to be safe from aggressors like porn and the corporate giants that seek to define his play in a way that isn't helpful to his mental and emotional development. Please give _____ (insert your son's name) a desire to be creative in his play. Help me to know the difference between desires and preferences he has that are from his personality (like preferring less active forms of creative play such as building things) and those that have become bad habits (like an overt obsession with the family computer).

From this day forward, I commit to creating opportunities for him to experience creative play so he can build the skill of self-control. Would you give his dad (my husband) a desire to enter into this process, and give me patience to let you be the one to motivate him? Help me to have the self-control to say "no" and be discerning in how I spend my time and money on him. Thanks for the chance that you've given me to play with my son today. In Jesus' Name, amen!

Budget-crunching ideas for indoor play

If you're a mom in the city who just can't get out, here are some fun mother–son dates that will release a little testosterone inside the house.

- *Balloon-swatting (ages 5 to 8).* Boys like to swat, kick, hit, karate chop…you get the idea. But if you're stuck inside, that can be complicated unless you have a cheap bag of latex balloons. Let him help you blow them up. Set up a few boundaries and let the swatting begin!

- *Box play (ages 8 to 10).* Boys really know how to think outside the box when they're in one. (Pun intended.) Keep your eyes open for a super-sized box or two from a friend's recently delivered appliance or furniture purchase. They're usually happy to get rid of them! Just set it up in a semiprivate spot and it'll become his own hideout, which the likes of Tom Sawyer could appreciate!

- *Build a fort (ages 11, 12).* This is no ordinary fort. You have to challenge him. Give him some manly tools from your husband's tool box. Think: clamps and vises, plastic tarps, bungee cords, and other big-guy stuff. Set him loose in your hallway, basement, or garage to build something truly incredible.

"For several years I had been very concerned that my middle son 'loved' computer games too much…Two years ago, he decided (on his own) to generally avoid playing computer games. He'll go months without touching one. This was after he read the book *PlayStation Nation*, which his dad gave him. The book was about kids getting addicted to gaming, and how it's a negative influence in their lives. He realized that he too easily got 'hooked' and that his computer gaming was becoming too important to him. THIS WAS AN ANSWER TO PRAYER!"

*Jen, mother of Chase, 15,
Dustin, 16, and Alex, 18*

CHAPTER 8

Way #2: Give Him a Book So He Can Discover a Real "Call of Duty"

M om, I need to talk to you," Robby's fifth-grade eyes made contact with mine and told me he had something very serious to tell me.

"Okay," I said, sitting at the little table crammed into the kitchen of our small rental house. "Shoot!"

"I can't read this book," he said, bringing it from behind his back and laying it on the table. Soberly, he pushed it toward me as if giving it back to me.

"Really?" I inquired. "Why?"

"It has bad things in it," he told me and went on to explain some rather dark and evil plot material.

"Could it be a battle between good and evil?" I asked. "Maybe good will win in the end?"

God's Way

"Speak up for those who cannot speak for themselves, for the rights of all who are destitute. Speak up and judge fairly; defend the rights of the poor and needy."

PROVERBS 31:8-9

CORE VALUES: HONOR, RESPONSIBILITY

"Mom, I don't think that evil is called evil in this book," he said. "I think the people who read it learn that evil can be used for good. That's why I have to ask you if I can do something."

"What's that?" I asked.

"I feel really bad that you paid so much for this book, but I don't think we can give it to someone else," he said and then paused. "I wouldn't want someone else to read it. I want to throw it away."

I grabbed the garbage can that was nearby and put it in front of him.

Robby plopped the book into it.

"It sounds like you've been a discerning reader today, Robby," I encouraged. "I'm really proud of you!"

He smiled and tore off down the hall to his bedroom. "Thanks, Mom!" he shouted in relief over his shoulder.

I reached down into that garbage can and picked up the book, intending to inspect it with a little reading of my own before I revisited the topic to discuss it with him.

Today's boys need a lot of discernment to navigate the books, video games, and other media created for and marketed to them. My research led me to a lot of things about how to raise a boy to become a man who cares about the needs of others. At first glance, these things may seem to be unrelated to each other, but if you'll give me a shot, I think I can prove to you that the books he reads and the games he plays will make or break the man you're molding. These choices directly affect how much time your son spends thinking about and seeking to please himself.

The Goal: Boys with Pure Religion

Before jumping into the fantasy world of books and gaming, let's keep the purpose in mind. Remember, we're trying to raise good boys to be good men, right? This includes helping your son 1) grow up to be the primary provider for a family he lovingly leads and 2) become a member of his community who seeks to do good and meet the needs of others.

Proverbs 31 isn't just for women, as I stated earlier. The first few verses admonish men to "speak up for those who cannot speak for themselves, for the rights of all who are destitute. Speak up and judge fairly; defend the rights of the poor and needy." James adds that men who defend widows and orphans have "pure religion." That's the goal: a grown son who not only does good but *is* good, to his core. But how do we get there?

Click here!

Go to wikipedia.com and search "list of classic children's books." Here you'll find a treasure trove of literary wealth to share with your boy!

Leaders Are Readers

I believe that teaching a boy to love reading—the right books, that is—is one of the foundational skills to becoming a good man who is a leader. Harry Truman once said, "Leaders are readers!" Reading is good and helps to build good men.

But since 1992, boys have continued to decline in both reading tests and their interest in education overall. Boys tend to score 10 to 20 points lower on standardized tests in reading and writing than girls. In the Maine Educational Assessment tests, girls bested boys' reading scores in 142 schools, while in only six schools did the boys take the girls.[1] Sadly, this trend can be seen in every state, and it seems to place boys on a trajectory *away* from higher education. While the college-age population is 50.7 percent male and 49.2 percent female, males comprise only 42.8 percent of the college population, with women the other 57.2 percent.[2]

This drop in performance is *not* just a simple difference between boys and girls. One of the greatest reasons we believe this has nothing to do with reading: Girls are kicking boy's hineys in math these days! This used to be the uncontested stronghold of the male brain. Today high-school girls outnumber boys two to one in "top 10 senior" rankings.[3] This new trend demonstrates a work-ethic change, not a recent dramatic evolution in the female brain.

Dennis and Barbara Rainey, whose work influenced our parenting of our tweens and teens, took time when they first started their family to write the top values they wanted their children to embrace. For

Barbara, one was "strong work ethic." The couple both embraced this goal, and they believed that it "did wonders for training our children to stay out of [the] trap of mediocrity."[4] That probably best sums up our concern about the decline in reading and interest in education among boys. While we don't think every boy needs or is best suited to go to college, we do believe every child needs a good solid work ethic and the ability to think critically.

Another reason we feel that the downward statistical spiral of boys' achievement in education is a work-ethic issue is the simple fact that the increasing disparity in educational success between boys and girls can be traced back to 1992. What happened about then?

Boy Meets Video Game

The first commercially viable video game was Computer Science, which came out in 1971. But the state of the technology confined gaming to a place that's now rather archaic: the arcade! Maybe you remember being allowed to slink off to one for a few minutes when you were 14 or 15. However, it wasn't long before we were caught up in the fast-paced—ha-ha—world of Atari. The games of Asteroids and Pong ruled the gaming world.

The 1980s was when gaming burst through the technology barriers with the advent of the first gaming system—Nintendo. And it was then that some computers were created with gaming in mind—the Commodore 64, the Macintosh, and PC compatibles. The minds of boys would never be the same.

Today a typical boy averages 35 hours per week in front of a screen. While a certain amount of television watching comes into play, for boys gaming systems and computer gaming will take up the majority of this time. I see three problems with this.

1. Boys aren't reading as much as they used to. Reading is the strongest predictor of school success.[5] Edward M. Hallowell, writing in *The Childhood Roots of Adult Happiness,* encourages us to "read aloud to your children for as long as they will let you...A recent study showed that two of the activities most closely correlated with high SAT scores were eating family dinner together and being read aloud to as a child."[6] If we are going to raise good boys who have the intellect for and an interest in being leaders, we have to give them good books to read and create an interest in reading them.

It has always been a harder job to get boys to read as opposed to girls. Michael Gurian says this is simply biology. Boys do less well in reading because they have a smaller *corpus callosum*—the part that connects the left and right hemisphere of the brain—and that makes reading harder. But he also goes on to say that biology equals proclivity. It does not equal destiny.[7] Boys spend far more time than girls plugged in to screens. But since we saw boys doing substantially better on reading tests before 1992 than we see them doing now, we have to assume that the decline is simply because something else has taken up their minds: gaming.

2. Boys are sleeping less. Parents are moving gaming systems, televisions, and computers into the rooms of their children during the elementary school or tween years. About 50 percent of boys have some kind of screen in their rooms. Almost as soon as that screen enters a boy's domain, a vicious cycle begins. Unrestricted access behind closed doors leads to a lot of unmonitored use. A lot of unmonitored use results in lack of sleep, which in turn hurts brain development. Is it really surprising, then, that boys are often having difficulty in school?

3. Boys are experiencing a false sense of purpose or mission. John Eldredge penned an entire book based around one simple concept. *Wild At Heart* struck deeply into the hearts of men and became a bestseller because adult men are struggling with their sense of purpose or mission in a society Eldredge says has "spent the last thirty years redefining masculinity into something more sensitive, safe, manageable, and well, feminine."[8] He says that every man needs a battle to fight, an adventure to live, and a beauty to save. Men need a mission!

Michael Gurian aptly titled a whole chapter in one of his books, "Your Son Needs to Save the World." The author calls this need a boy's "sacred mission." We've termed it his "call of duty." You can see this need in little boys in the same way you can see little girls' need to be beautiful, when they play dress-up as preschoolers.

As I write this, a three-year-old boy in my church has been wearing a homemade cape and sword everywhere he goes. After seeing him like this several times, I finally asked if he was "Superman." He wasted no time drawing his sword and shouting to me that he was, in fact, "Bible Man!" (Yahoo!)

From a very young age, boys want to conquer something. They need this. They were created for it. This need becomes more consuming between the ages of eight and ten. At this stage, a boy is trying to become the master of his world, and he'll make no bones about telling you so.

Gaming, however, gives him a false sense of purpose (and up to 25 percent of boys will actually become addicted to that sensation). Achieving the next level in the game Call of Duty sends a message to his brain that he's found a sacred purpose. In the real world, he's sitting on his bed way past bedtime, thwarting his ability to answer to a real, lifelong call of duty.

A dad's confession
by Bob

My biggest regret as a father is buying that first PlayStation console. As a dad, I knew it was the coolest toy ever. I reveled in the delight of my son when he opened that final box on Christmas morning.

Video games are a phenomenal way to escape into another world. I know that on the occasional night I myself became a virtual soldier. I could retreat for hours into the game. Dannah called me for dinner, and I didn't even listen until she really, really called me. It was hard to break away. I liked the isolation, not just the competition.

And that's what I find to be most sinister about today's gaming world: the isolation.

Years ago when I was playing Pong, it was a two-player game. Today all the popular games are one-player games or games you can play through the Internet with some faceless, nameless person. Either way, they isolate our boys.

Cultivating a Real Call of Duty

And here is probably the most insidious danger of gaming. You don't want your son to miss out on his real life mission because he has spent the most formative years of his life locked into completing fantasy missions. It *is* possible in this day and age to raise sons who will take on the desperate problems of the world.

While I was writing this, I was at one of the most exhilarating church services of my life. One of the things that touched my passion buttons was that my dear friend Pastor Paul Grabill shared the ministries of his adult sons who were visiting for the weekend. Ryan is working with the organization Convoy of Hope as a disaster relief coordinator. He was a first responder to the horrific Joplin, Missouri, tornado in 2011. His is a face that would make me feel safe and loved were I in a place of devastation. (What a call of duty!) His big brother, Rob (wife, Ireida), is a missionary in India, where he is fighting on the front line of villages where families sell their girls to survive. Somehow, I can see Rob kicking down a brothel door one day. (Again, what a call of duty!) These are "pure religion" men. And it exhilarated me to see Paul and his wife, Arline, get to see the fruit of raising good boys.

I won't try to chart your son's future for you in this book. He may be the world's next great computer programmer, building a bank account to fund good works globally, or he may be an athlete with a testimony for Christ that resurrects our hope in good sportsmanship. Whatever his call, the root of any life call is found in valuing hard work *so he can meet the needs of others*.

Give Him a Book

How do we get our son to this place? Let's start with reading, since that seems to predict so much about his future ability to work hard in school and in life. Here are a few ideas to help you get your son reading instead of playing with a controller.

Let him be a part of choosing reading material that he likes, by simply exposing him to books. When my son was a young reader, his Mom-mom

(Bob's mother) gave us an old box of his dad's books. Robby quickly absorbed Beverly Cleary's Ralph the Mouse trilogy: *The Mouse and the Motorcycle, Runaway Ralph,* and *Ralph S. Mouse.* I kept bringing that box out to see which of Bob's old books would capture Robby's interest and, in a way, connect them as father and son. Each time the box came out, it was memory lane for dad and a new reading challenge for our son.

When he was a little older, the books I had read at that stage were more co-ed in nature. It was my turn to get to enjoy my love of reading. It was so fun to talk about my old favorites as he read my worn-out copies of *A Wrinkle in Time* by Madeleine L'Engle, *Where the Red Fern Grows* by Wilson Rawls, *The Cay* by Theodore Taylor, and *The Lion, the Witch and the Wardrobe* by C.S. Lewis.

Random Bob Thought:

These are good books!

Especially "Runaway Ralph."

You don't have to have a box of old books to share your passion—a trip to the library to explore will do just fine. My kids loved the library visits we made when they were young. When they got older, I'd take them to the bookstore the first week of summer and give them a budget to buy books for summer reading challenges, which always offered some kind of reward. (One mom interviewed for this book said she paid her sons $100 per summer if they read ten books. It worked!)

Does this seem like a struggle? You yourself may not love reading—or your son may not. It's okay to lure him in with *Garfield* and the Sunday funnies. You might get him a subscription to a magazine that favors his interest and has good writing. *Discover* (for the scientist in your son) and *SI [Sports Illustrated] Kids* (for the athletic boy) have great articles that offer a shorter read. But don't simply ignore the need for him to read, and be sure to press past easy reading (like comics) to something more challenging. And as you progress, make sure you move past all the mindless "booger" and "fart" books out there.

Give him the right kinds of books. There's good news. There's bad news. The good news is that we know boys need to read more and efforts are being made to address the issue. The bad news is that many of the well-intentioned people who want to help them achieve lifelong success are creating books that are either mindless drivel or capable of confusing his code of honor. So…

> *Random Bob Thought:*
>
> *I have ADD.*
>
> *I love books.*
>
> *Your son can too.*

- *Avoid too many books that exploit flatulence and "grossology."* Maybe you've heard of Captain Underpants or the Butt Books. Perhaps you have a copy of the new classic *Sir Fartsalot Hunts the Booger*. These books have been published in an effort to meet boys where they are, and while a copy or two won't kill all his brain cells I am fairly certain that the dumbing down of the English language won't increase his vocab.

  I also don't think they're a great element in raising *good* boys. (Do we really want our sons to stay trapped in a seventh-grade bodily-functions obsessed brain? Are the best role models for our sons found in a book titled *Sweet Farts*?) One *Wall Street Journal* writer lamented,

  > *One obvious problem with the* Sweet Farts *philosophy of education is that it is more suited to producing a generation of barbarians and morons than to raising the sort of men who make good husbands, fathers and professionals. If you keep meeting a boy where he is, he doesn't go very far.* [9]

  I am not saying that the Gresh home didn't carry a copy or two of these kinds of books. (In fact, the kids rather enjoyed the stand-up comedy routines their dad

Random Bob Thought: You have to admit, that's a funny title... at least dads think so.

built around Captain Underpants.) I'm just saying they should be the exception, not the rule, in regard to what your son reads.

- *Avoid books that blur the lines between good and evil.* While we realize there's a lot of debate to be had over books like the Harry Potter series or even perhaps The Lord of the Rings trilogy, it seems clear to us that the book industry has gone crazy over publishing tales of evil and that often the authors do not clearly categorize evil as evil. There are "good" vampires for our daughters to lust after, and "good" witches for our sons to idealize. Be careful! The Bible says witchcraft is evil and is opposed to a proper dependence on God himself. Galatians 5:20 lists it as one of the signs of the sinful nature. In many places it is condemned in the strongest of language. We should never take anything to do with witches, vampires, or darkness lightly, especially if it is not clearly spelled out that it is evil.

In the scenario at the beginning of the chapter, it was a copy of the first Harry Potter book that Robby brought me to throw away. I was humbled at his...well, his goodness. He demonstrated a concern for his friends when he threw it away rather than giving it away. And when I looked in the pages I could see clearly what he did—the lines between good and evil were blurred. Since he told me that he liked the book and the style of it, I handed him a copy of the Lord of the Rings trilogy, which seems to me at least a little more clear about good being good and evil being evil. He devoured it...three times! (I do realize that even this series has areas that are debatable in regard to good or bad messages.)

The point is not to ban books—and I'm not banning Harry. The point is to be discerning about what you read because *anything* we expose ourselves to informs what we believe and how we live. While the world tries to tell you— the parent—that it's just fiction and won't hurt a thing, God says that there is good and evil, right and wrong, truth and lies. He doesn't blur the lines, nor should we in these tender years while our children are learning the skill of discernment.

Give him books that push him to be more than he is. Gone are the days when it was easy to find books that contained lead characters that were men of honor. We are no longer publishing biographies of presidents, soldiers, and missionaries. But that's what our boys need, so look hard!

In presenting our sons with reading that offers good role models, we override the natural human tendency toward complacency and begin to train them to have a taste for excellence. C.S. Lewis once wrote,

> *The little human animal will not at first have the right responses. It must be trained to feel pleasure, liking, disgust, and hatred at those things which really are pleasant, likeable, disgusting, and hateful.*

Your son isn't going to pick up a copy of *Tom Sawyer* and automatically appreciate it as a piece of classic literature. A taste must be developed. Press on to introduce him to more challenging forms and styles as he is an older tween.

For example, when Robby was a middle-schooler he began to enjoy the Christian-based supernatural thrillers of Frank Peretti, like *This Present Darkness*. When Peretti came out with a fascinating autobiography on his younger years and what he suffered at the hands of bullies, I was quick to buy it and share it with Robby. During those years, my friend Suzy encouraged him to read *I Know Why the Caged Bird Sings* by Maya Angelou during a trip our family took to Africa. There he'd be seeing the root of what she wrote about in her struggle to overcome racism. I hope these were experiences that created a hunger for self-help, biographies, and books that deal with modern-day issues. Who knows, maybe one of those issues we introduced him to will be a place where the seed of goodness will grow into a real-life call of duty!

And that's the key, isn't it? We're just tending the soil where God will plant a life purpose for our sons. What kind of soil are you cultivating in your son's heart?

Reading Between the Lines

I really do believe that one of the secrets to raising a good boy is rather simple: Turn the video games off and give him a good book to read. Yes, it's countercultural to raise a boy this way. Am I saying that your son should never see an Xbox? Never have the chance to help an Italian-American plumber named Mario exterminate the pesky Fighter Flies and Shellcreepers that emerge from the New York City sewers? Never learn about ports and how to use "gamerisms"—the lingo of the world of video gaming? Believe it or not, I'd be flying in the face of research if I took a hard line like that. There's a great deal of research to indicate that *some* gaming can be good for our sons. In all the debate I see two valid arguments in favor of gaming.

1. Video games even the playing field. It could be that your son might not excel at sports, but he's a worthy competitor with a controller in his hand. Michael Gurian notes that "a less physical boy may be like a madman when he turns on his computer."[10] He calls gaming a "channeling activity" that allows a boy who isn't the fastest, strongest, or best athlete to activate testosterone, drive, and positive risk behaviors.

Robby used this same reasoning with me recently when we were talking about gaming and my concern that we'd allowed him too much time with a controller in his hand. He said, "I think the biggest reason guys like them is the competition factor. It's an outlet where the games can create competition even if you're not tops on the playing fields outside or on a court."

Not having an ounce of a competitive spirit in my bones, I don't really get that. But I think it's important for a mom to step back and understand that winning once in a while feels to a boy like finding a great pair of shoes feels to a girl—adrenaline rush! It might not be the wisest use of my hour, but as long as those shoes are within budget, "No harm, no foul!" That's basketball lingo, Mom. It means that if an action has no result on the end of the game, there should be no penalty. Read between the lines: Maybe sometimes a little bit of gaming is okay, if it's not going to impact the final outcome of our good son, huh?

Singled moms

What games are good?

"You are the only one who can decide what your children should be exposed to, and you can't loosen up on your standards to make up for what they've lost in their family structure. I'm making our home, which I call the haven where the Holy Spirit is, a protected place of integrity. It *matters* what goes into your eyes and your heart. I might have the protection too tight, and if the Lord shows me how to loosen up I'm gonna do that. My boys have had a PlayStation, but until just a few years ago they had only E-rated games. They're kinda the dorkiest games, but I don't care."

—Angela Thomas

2. Video games may foster visual–spatial skills. Perhaps you've read articles about how boys who play video games tend to have a leg up in critical hand-eye coordination problem-solving careers like engineering or surgery. One reason may be that in the higher-education classroom, these two fields use virtual methods to teach. Another may be that the experience actually builds up the brain to be able to reason more quickly. Either way, this idea of faster problem-solving skills found its way into my son's line of reasoning when we discussed gaming.

"Think of it like playing chess, Mom," he said to me, making clear to me that we both held the premise that chess enjoys the approval of the most educated, "but with more people and more places. I have to solve the problem faster than my opponent. It's a greater level of problem-solving than chess." And just in case I wasn't buying his argument, he added, "And I killed it in school."

In fact, he's "killing it" in an honors-level engineering program. (Hmm?) Later in our conversation he explained to me "one more time" how the physical vapor deposition system he's using to vaporize…uh, er…stuff works. Then he excused himself from lunch because he needed to go repair it. (How's the kid know how to repair something when I can't even remember its name?)

He had me.

A No-Regrets Plan for Controlling Gaming

While, looking back, I am uncomfortable with how many hours of gaming we allowed, I didn't ruin my son by buying him a PlayStation. Here are a few words of advice from a mom who, if she had another chance, would have pulled back a bit, but doesn't regret the gaming altogether:

1. *Set limits in terms of overall screen time.* With so many screens to choose from, it's easier and wiser to just set an overall screen-time limit. (This also gives your son the responsibility to prioritize which screen or screens he will use for his allotment that specific day. Should he use his computer to access his math assignment and teacher help, or should he use his gaming system to fight another epic—but very virtual—battle?)

    Taking into account that he needs an average of ten hours of sleep during his tween years (yes, t-e-n!) and should have an hour a day minimum of exercise/outdoor play, most experts suggest a limit of between one and two hours a day. This will bring his screen time way down from the average 38 hours per week per child to something like 7 to 14 hours! That's radical. And radical is what our culture needs to reclaim "goodness."

2. *Learn how the video ratings system works, and communicate your family preferences.* The Entertainment Software Rating Board (ESRB) requires games to be marked with one of six ratings. They are EC, E, E10+, T, M, and AO. Here's how they break down.

> EC = suitable for children aged 3+
> E = suitable for children aged 6+
> E10+ = suitable for children aged 10+
> T = suitable for children aged 13+
> M = suitable for children aged 17+
> AO = Adults only

You can learn more about the ratings system at esrb.com, and review the basic reasons for the ratings given to specific games (or new versions). For example, Call of Duty is the bestselling line of games of all time as I'm writing this. Call of Duty: Roads to Victory, one of its versions, is given a T rating and cited for "blood, language, violence."

3. *As your son gets older, allow him more self-monitoring of his gaming.* When Robby was a tween, he had very little say about how much time he was allowed to spend on his gaming system: One hour a day was our family limit. He got two hours a day on weekends. Recently he told me that this sometimes made him angry. (Prepare to be the bad guy!)

But as he grew older, his responsibilities helped him self-monitor. As a member of his school's soccer and basketball teams, he rarely made it home before six o'clock on a practice night. (Ten on a game night.) And he still had homework to do, so he didn't have many nights where he had more than an hour of gaming. Today, he is in his own apartment and enjoys gaming with his roommates for an hour or so a day but says that allowing him to self-monitor in high school is what keeps him limiting his time today. And "we're not playing enough to be at the top of the playing pool, Mom. There are guys out there who do nothing but play, and they eat our shorts!" (That makes me happy!)

Whew! That was our toughest chapter to write. Was it a tough one for you to read? Hopefully, you'll be able to learn from our regret in this area of gaming and book-reading! Let's hurry on to a topic where the Gresh Family fares a bit better: wing nites and fantasy football. Who doesn't like wings? Let us show you how they can build a "good" man!

His Way

Take a few moments to prayerfully write three goals you have in terms of your son's reading and video game playing. Perhaps you need to be more careful with the hours of time he spends gaming, or the kinds of games he plays. Maybe God is calling you to a challenge of having him read more than he plays? Or having him earn his playtime with reading? Be creative. He's your son. Not ours. You know him best and you know what he needs.

_____

_____

_____

_____

_____

_____

_____

_____

_____

_____

_____

_____

Prayer for honor and responsibility
based on Proverbs 31:8-9

Lord, I deeply desire to raise a son who is full of honor and who rises to the responsibility of his manhood. Please help me to have eyes to see what critical decisions I need to make while he is young, so he can be this man when he is grown.

I ask you to make _____ (insert your son's name) a man who speaks up for those who cannot speak for themselves. I ask you to make him one who defends the rights of the destitute. Help him to be one who will speak up and judge fairly. I know that to be this man he must be connected to his world rather than isolated, and diligent in his studies so he can think critically.

Please, Lord, help me to teach my son to love to learn and read. And help me to know what to say "no" to in this world that would like to make him more focused on his own desires than the needs of others. I ask for wisdom in your holy Name, amen.

"My greatest concern about raising boys is 'no father in the home—either physically or mentally checked out.' My husband was involved, but I wish he had been so much more involved. He is a workaholic, and there was a period of time when he worked and lived in a different town in order to put the boys in Christian school. He spent the weekends with us. I think it was a big mistake because the boys needed him more than just on the weekends."

Pam, mother of adult sons Corey and Micah

CHAPTER 9

Way #3:
Host Wing Nites and
Fantasy Football Parties

Robby, you've made Mom's minivan stink!" accused a never-at-a-loss-for-truth fourth-grade Lexi.

Sitting behind the wheel up front, I was alarmed at her direct nature. *Okay, maybe she got that from me,* I thought. She'd certainly heard me complain about the smell of my white minivan for the past week. It did stink!

"I don't smell anything," answered a stuffy-nosed Robby.

"I do. I smell…" Lexi began loudly taking in whiff after whiff. Looking back at her through the rearview mirror, I could see her thinking after each sniff.

God's Way

"He who walks with the wise grows wise, but a companion of fools suffers harm."

PROVERBS 13:20

CORE VALUES: PURPOSE, COMMUNITY

As she worked on her definitive description of the deadly scent, I had the ironic thought that I was terribly delighted it smelled so bad. After all, the cause was a boyhood rite-of-passage trip. Robby had gone away to Space Camp in Huntsville, Alabama. Fourteen hours away from home with not a friend to his name as he began, he'd experienced liftoff at 4 G's and weightlessness. He'd even captained the takeoff of a simulated space-shuttle mission.

Random Bob Thought: Teach your kid to use deodorant very early on.

As a reward for all his hard work—there was a lot of math to do between missions—his dad, his youth pastor, Don Jones, and his best friend Bart loaded into my minivan to go pick him up. Then they looped over to the rapids of the Ocoee River, which boasts being the site of the 1996 Olympic whitewater competitions. They would also be the rapids that the two best friends, along with Robby's dad and youth pastor, conquered. Afterward, they loaded back into that white minivan in all their whitewater glory and let the damp scent of wet clothes and river water soak into every fiber of my carpet and upholstery.

"Wild!" I suddenly said.

"What?" asked Lexi.

"It smells wild," I said matter-of-factly. "Robby, Bart, Dad, and Pastor Don were wild, and that's what it smells like."

I could see Robby quietly nodding with an almost-there grin on his face.

"Nah," grumbled Lexi. "It just smells like Robby's wet socks."

That too, I thought.

Parenting a tween boy is full of olfactory memories, if ya know what I (Bob) mean. It seemed that every time Robby took off on an adventure there was a wild scent to remind us of it in the days following. From the smell of his hiking boots after a week at Camp K to the smell of Dannah's white minivan after the Ocoee River trip, we were often nose deep in wild.

The fact is, our boys need a little bit of physical adventure to discover their purpose and to have an outlet for the desire to take risks and be aggressive. Since moms—as a general rule—like life neat and safe and are more risk-adverse, you mothers may not be the best teachers of purpose to our sons. (I know, I know! Lots of stereotypes in those last few sentences. Remember, we're working with averages here. Maybe you're the mom who will skydive for her sixtieth birthday like my brave mom... And she's promising to do it again with me to celebrate her seventieth.) In general, a dad will understand a boy's need for understanding himself by discovering purpose, and that could get a little...uh, "wild."

Let him be wild

"As a pediatrician, I've seen plenty of boys with broken arms, spider bites, or who have scraped a knee playing soldier in the woods. But these are just part of growing up. Too many of us parents obsess about healthy diversions that active boys like to do, while not recognizing what is truly dangerous for our boys—like popular music, television, and video games that deaden their sensibilities, shut them off from real human interaction, impede the process of maturation, prevent them from burning up energy in useful outdoor exercise, divorce them from parents, and lower their expectations of life."

—Dr. Meg Meeker, *Boys Should Be Boys*[1]

The "Wolfing" Process

Let me introduce you to the concept of *wolfing*.[2] (I've never been near a wolf, but I'd bet they smell wild.) I was first introduced to the wolfing model in my late twenties by a dear friend and Christian counselor named Kaye Briscoe King. Here's how it looks.

Wolves are raised in two distinct stages. In stage one, the first five to six weeks of life, the little cubs are sheltered and nurtured by the mother. During this time, they stay in the den and, until about the third week or so, are rarely seen by the rest of the pack. Before that, the mother is teaching them to be intimate—she cuddles with them—and safe—she takes care of them and teaches them to bathe, eat, and rest.

At about six weeks, the growing cubs come out of the den and begin to learn about risk and purpose. Dad steps in to teach them, primarily using a tree branch to play a kind of relay game. Dad carries the stick. Cub carries the stick. Dad carries it. Cub carries it. Along the way, the dad is leading the growing wolf farther and farther away from the security of the den. But there's intent in the game: He's teaching the youngster to hunt. Wolves, you see, hunt for survival. It is their primary purpose. In teaching the cub to risk and to play, dad teaches it to have purpose. All the while, mom is still safely in the den available for more training in nurture when her little pack comes back from wildlife lessons with dad.

In the end, wolves live in packs—in community—and hunt. That's it. They know each other and they know their purpose. And mom and dad work together to instill those two values into them.

I want to propose that *wolfing*—a cooperative effort in parenting—is essential to raise a son who will be capable of authentic community and who lives a life of good purpose.

Now, *purpose* is one of those great big, vague words that have multiple meanings. Unlike wolf cubs, our sons don't need to hunt to survive—after all, there is a McDonald's on practically every corner! A boy's purpose, I believe, will include being a contributor to society, being intimate with a wife in a lifelong marriage, being a great father, and continuing to grow in the nurture and admonition of the Lord at every stage of the way.

As your son grows from being a "cub"—those preschool and early elementary years—the parenting process will naturally require Dad to be more involved, especially as your son seeks to learn what to do with all his "risk-taking" hormones and how to direct them toward a fulfilling life purpose.

Singled moms

How do you have a relationship with your children's father?

"What I've decided about Christian marriages is this: The devil has really had to do some dirty things between two parents to bring them to divorce. It's never the best choice. I walked out into divorce under the authority of my pastor and elders. They told me, 'You have to leave!' Not many churches know how to do this. I lived as a single mom for the better part of ten years and was under the protection of my elders during that time. Occasionally I'll come across a woman who is divorced and has a great relationship with her former husband, but the reality is that it is very rare. You should not beat yourself up for it, but do your best to live in as much harmony as you can."

—Angela Thomas

Wolf Mom

Our son is over six feet tall these days, but as we've said before, he's still a huge cuddler. He never fails to wrap his huge arms around me, Dannah, when he greets me. He even "cuddles" his teenage sisters, drawing their heads against his shoulders and wrapping his hands up over their heads. There his hands "tap-tap-tap" their hair softly. I love to see this (I have a picture of it on my cell phone). I taught him how to do that when he was little—and I taught him well.

By his tweens, your job as a mom to teach him intimacy in a tactile way is usually over. And we'll deal with how you continue to teach him safety and body care in the next chapter. In this chapter, I would really like to focus on how you empower the Wolf Dad in your son's life.

Let your son venture out with Dad. A Wolf Dad has to be strong and unafraid. He teaches his son to go out into the world and hunt down his purpose, but to live inside the lines of proper behavior. He pushes his son to become an independent risk-taker so he can find purpose. He does this best by just being with him...taking him farther and farther from home on adventures. (It takes a lot of playing to teach wise risk-taking.) On the flip side, if a Wolf Dad sees a son behaving in a manner that would risk the safety his Wolf Mom has taught him, the Wolf Dad is man enough to growl…loudly.

One of the most unique stories about this characteristic of wolves appeared in a book we read, entitled *The Man Who Lives with Wolves*. It chronicles the amazing experience of Shaun Ellis, who lived near a wolf pack to study their behavior and was actually accepted into it. He was treated like something of an adolescent pup who needed to be "trained" by the wolf dads of the pack.

During a pack hunt, Shaun and one of the male wolves were left behind to guard the den, which was full of new pups. After a few hours, Shaun became thirsty and began to walk away from the den toward the nearby stream. The wolf jumped in front of him and snarled dangerously, backing him against a tree stump, where he held him against his will for a few hours. Later in the evening, the wolf finally relented, and Shaun began to walk to the stream, only to find evidence of a grizzly bear— known to rip apart wolves and humans alike. The bear had obviously spent a good amount of time eating, sleeping and…well, other things bears do that make it obvious they were there…on the path where he'd have walked. A Wolf Dad (whether four-legged or two) knows when to push and when to punish, and he's not afraid to growl!

Random Bob Thought:

Do not try this at home!

My man was and is a great Wolf Dad. I've watched him push Robby out of the comfort of safety to learn to risk. He's also never afraid to discipline our sweet boy in truth if he ever steps outside the bounds of safe behavior in his adventures. Bob was intentional and smart about how he connected to our son through play-adventures during his tween years, and he was unflinching in his resolve to keep Robby safe by punishing him if the need arose. (Thankfully, for Robby, it rarely did.)

Keep your paws away! I see a lot of dads in the process of being just as great as Bob was and is as a father…but with wives who are nagging the wild manhood right out of them! And that's what I feel God would have me address with you in this chapter, sweet mom. It's time we stopped nagging.

I've already shared with you that Bob took Robby out for wings every Thursday night during his tween years, and that I was constantly trying to involve myself in the conversation. There was a sense of nagging supervision in my approach as I asked question after question trying to check up on the progress of my boy. I was very supportive of the fact that they went, but Bob always had to Wolf Dad *me* when I tried to micromanage.

Trying to insert yourself into the games of manhood isn't the only way a mom can nag. I've seen other dads try to do something like Wing Nite, only to be nagged by a mom who "feels abandoned." This kind of nagging usually emasculates a man by making him simply stay home. Let them go! And then tell your husband—or your son's father—that he's doing a great job. Leave it at that.

Am I saying you can never suggest that your husband needs to talk to your son about sex, or take him on the upcoming father–son camping trip at church, or teach him to shave? No. I'm just saying that you should 1) wait a while to let him figure it out before you offer gentle encouragement, 2) let him do it his way (not yours), and 3) do a lot more *affirming* than nagging.

Here's where a little confession needs to come into play: I'm not the world's poster wife when it comes to being a helpmate. I want to be a helper, but I'm full of myself and my ambition and my ideas and my opinions. Me! Me! Me! (And all this studying about being "good"—outwardly focused toward the needs of others—is challenging my heart to step up.) I can be a terrible follower of my husband. I often fail to consider his emotions when I am barging into a season of life with the intention of taking it by the horns. While there were times he needed my encouragement (read: reminding *without* nagging) about something that needed to happen between him and Robby, most of the time the most valuable contribution I could make was simply encouraging him when he took the lead.

Let him keep them safe. The hardest time for me to let him lead was when his Wolf Dad personality bared its teeth to discipline our children back to safety. I remember the time that Robby said something disrespectful to me when we were putting the Christmas decorations away above our garage. Wolf Dad came out and growled an invitation to Robby to read the tragically long biography *DAWS: The Story of Dawson Trotman, Founder of the Navigators,* and to then write a report on how Trotman displayed character. I felt it was too much on the last day of Robby's Christmas vacation. I remember advocating for something easier.

Random Bob Thought:
I love Dawson Trotman, but that was a 300-page bio...not the first choice of a boy!

A few years later, Lexi followed in her brother's footsteps. A word of disrespect toward me resulted in her copying out every single word in the book of Proverbs. The pile of tissues in her bedroom got higher and higher as each hour of writing went on, and I just couldn't stand the drama.

In situations like these, I'd sometimes try to get Bob alone to "explain" my point of view. I regret that. I wish I had been more affirming of his decisions in these cases.

When it was less dramatic—like the time he dropped Autumn, who could not overcome her stubborn fear of swimming, into the middle of a lake with nothing but her life jacket and Stormie, our wonder dog—I was often vocal *in front* of the kids!

I regret my lack of affirmation of my husband. I'm learning to be better at it. And I now know that he was really doing great things in our kids' lives.

Recently Robby told me this:

> *I didn't like reading that very long book and writing that report on the last day of my Christmas break, when I wanted to be having fun! It was something I never wanted to do again. But I learned that you don't always get in trouble for doing bad things in our house if you're honest about it. You get in trouble for disrespect and dishonesty. That's when the big discipline kicked in, and I didn't want to experience that so I just didn't talk back. At first it was because I didn't want to be disciplined, but eventually I learned that it was a good way to behave in life.*

Wow! I guess he'll remember the life lesson of reading that book more than he'd have remembered a few more hours of free time on that cold January day, huh?

Were there times when Bob was too strong in his discipline? Yes. And I have wonderful memories of him self-adjusting. Lexi never finished writing Proverbs…alone. Her dad sat beside her, and they took turns writing the last half of the book, verse by verse, until the consequence was fulfilled. And that time he threw Autumn into the lake? At dinner tonight she told me that, yes, she had been frightened, but it was an exhilarating feeling when she found the end of the water and rose up alive and well out of it!

Wolf Dads aren't bullies. They're *compassionate toward* their children and *passionate about* raising them to be good. There's a difference, and a true Wolf Dad has a heart that's soft when he's been too strong.

Here's the problem: All too often these days, Wolf Dads are muzzled by women who mean their children and their marriage no harm, but who are actually doing a great deal of damage as they dismantle the picture of family that God says is the ideal. Hint: It includes a word that's tough to swallow, and it starts with an "s." Practicing submission is a great way to see if there is a Wolf Dad hiding under your nagging.

Wolf Dad

I, Bob, think I should step back in here. (This would be a great time to hand this book to your son's dad for a few brief paragraphs.) The whole concept of wolfing revolutionized my thinking as a man and father. It showed me I was called out to be the one to teach my son to take risks and find his purpose.

In the word picture of the father wolf taking the cub out to play relay, you can see a type of rite of passage taking place. The cub is marked out as ready for a new stage of maturity by going out with dad on a great adventure. First dad carries the responsibility, then he passes it to his son, and so on, back and forth. The great adventure I created for my son included a whole lot of barbecue sauce (and a little bit of heartburn), taking a little risk on some Apple Computer stock, and camping in the mountains of Northern California. Let me explain how I "played relay" with my son.

Wing Nites were a mini-initiation into maturity that told Robby he was becoming a man. When I first told Robby we were going to go out for wings every Thursday night at nine o'clock, his eyes were wide as saucers.

"Nine o'clock!" he said. "That's almost bedtime, Dad!"

"Yep, but not on Thursday nights, Robster," I answered. "From now on, it's Wing Nite!"

And so began our relay.

Since I was new at this, I used a crutch at first. Armed with a copy of *Teknon and the Champion Warriors Mission Guide,* we set off to learn together. It's a great study that covers all the big, bad topics needed for a man's rite of passage: sex, money, integrity, honesty, hard work. Some weeks we went by the book, others we just ate wings—but it gave me something to lean on to keep a conversation rolling. Well, the conversation was rolling *sometimes*. Talking isn't the most critical element in father–son connection. Just *being* is what counts most. Be with him. Show him what a man looks like.

If you're going to talk about anything with him, make it money and sex. These two things seem to have the ability to rip a man's purpose right out from under him if they're not mastered with character. Here are two things I did as rites of passage to help Robby in those areas.

Trust your son with your money. Trust is a big rite of passage for a guy. (Michael Gurian writes about "Jack and the Beanstalk" being a mission of trust. When the mom sends the boy out to buy eggs, she is *trusting* him with a mission and with her money. Gurian makes a big fat hairy psychological deal of it all, which makes me think he's right on target.) When Robby was an older tween, I wanted him to sense that I trusted him with finances.

I am a Dave Ramsey guy. I believe one of the most important skills we can give any of our kids is money management, including teaching them the terror of debt. I required all of our kids to take the teen version of Ramsey's "Financial Peace University" course.

About the time Robby went through the course, I gave him $300 to invest in the stock market. (It was a lot of money to us. We didn't have much in savings at the time. I wanted Robby to learn lessons about money that I hadn't learned at his age, so I took a risk in giving him what I felt was a lot.) No strings attached. I was trusting him to do with it what he thought was wise and reasonable. I specifically wanted him to stretch himself, but to also make sure that the risk he took was wise and well-calculated. The boy chose Apple. Would you believe that at the time of this writing his shares were worth $11,000?

Lesson learned.

Since then, we've revisited money management lessons together, and I'm proud to see how my son saves, spends, and earns.

Set apart a time to talk about sex so your son learns how sacred it should be in his life. Your son will face a lifelong battle with lust in this sex-saturated world of ours. He can win, but he's got to be prepared. It's really important not to brush over the sex talks, but to make them stand out as memorable experiences. (And I do mean experiences…as in plural. This isn't a conversation you can get through while you sip on one Diet Coke.)

Our conversation started when Robby was a few days shy of being ten years old. (I'll let Dannah tell you about that in the next chapter.) My "set apart" conversation happened on a camping trip. It wasn't a huge ceremony or long conversation, but during that week, Robby and I signed a contract in which he promised to live a life of sexual purity. Dannah framed it when we brought it home and hung it next to his bed so he'd see it frequently and could remember his promise when he felt lonely or tempted.

I believe those three things— Wing Nites, the money to invest, and a week to call him to purity— were each critical stops on the journey in raising Robby to be good. But it isn't as easy as it looks. I had to be intentional in blocking out the time and staying focused. One thing I did not expect was that good people would have a hard time realizing that this appointment with my son—as important as any late-running board meeting might be, or a budget that was due the next day, or a personal problem a friend might be having— was unbreakable. But Dannah and I were resolved together to protect it. And now I have a young adult son who makes me so proud and honored to have shared those experiences with him.

Set apart for holy sex

Sex is God's holy gift of intimacy. Because of this, we suggest you create a very set-apart time when your son is an older tween or young teen to specifically ask him to live a life of purity. I, Bob, took Robby to JH Ranch, and I highly recommend their Father–Son Adventure Camp. They'll help you through the conversation because it's built right into their curriculum. But you don't have to spend a lot of money on a weekend like this. You can plan it yourself using FamilyLife's *Passport to Purity* if your son is in middle school. If your son is 14 or older, we recommend *Who Moved the Goalpost?: 7 Winning Strategies in the Sexual Integrity Game Plan* by none other than Bob and Dannah Gresh!

Wolfing As a Pack

If you're a single mom right now, you may be feeling lonely. But I (Dannah) assure you that this chapter is filled with a whole lot of promise for you. While nothing can quite replace the role of a father in a child's life, being a part of a larger community of men seems to be of primary significance for a boy. A boy will gravitate toward his own "tribe"—a gang or sports team, for example—if parents are not intentional in directing him toward one that supports their values. A mom and dad can work together, or independently, to be intentional about introducing their son to positive forms of community. This is good news for a mom who is raising a son without the help of a father.

One of the best stories I heard about the power of a male community to fill the void in a fatherless son was about a 16-year-old named Adrian Allen. Adrian wore a pair of dangling Uzi submachine gun earrings because he thought they were "nice." His left shoulder was tattooed with a greenish black "Q" in remembrance of his cousin, Quentin, who was serving life for killing a police officer.

"I'm not going to see him no more," said Adrian. "We did everything together."

Quentin *was* Adrian's community. But now he had been taken from him.

Adrian began to meet with a men's group for school support, guidance and…well, community. The program was run by a local teen health center at Adrian's high school.

"It's changed my life," Adrian says. He's become more assertive about communicating and making good decisions. He's starting to succeed in life. He's traded in his Uzi earrings for a classier set of diamond studs.

Community rescued him.

Don't wait until your son—fatherless or not—needs to be rescued to get him into an intentional community. There are two places where you can find who you are looking for.

Initiate him into the adult male community of your extended family. In many cases, your extended family will share your value system. Grandfathers, uncles, and cousins are valuable tools to shape your son's manhood.

When Robby was in middle school, he began to work for his "Grampy" at FireOne, my mom and dad's international pyrotechnics choreography company. (My dad helps the stuff that blows up in the sky on the Fourth of July look prettier by matching it within a tenth of a second to a musical score.) Not only was starting a job a rite of passage for our son, but it connected him to his grandfather. Again, most of their time was not spent talking about deep things. But his grampy has helped him form a sense of what a man is by simply letting him watch his life. (It's also aided in teaching him about finances. By the time Robby was out of high school, he had $7000 in the bank. He rarely spent a penny of what he earned in working five years of summers, weekends, and holidays.)

Maybe there's no family business in your extended family. Is there a passion for the Pittsburgh Steelers? (Okay! Dallas Cowboys?) Maybe your son can start to go on weekend trips with the guys. How about hunting? Having the male extended family members take your son out during deer season when he's old enough is a wonderful way to allow him to be "one of the guys." Are the men in your clan board gamers? Card players? Fishermen? Think creatively and you'll find ways to get your boy near good men in your family. And if good men in your immediate and extended family are scarce...

Initiate him into the adult male community of your faith. Raising a "good" son requires a lot of character. No better place to form that than in the accountability of Christian men. (Remember, more than females, males rely on external sources of accountability to monitor self-control and character. This is especially true of tween and teen boys, but a guy never really outgrows this need since he is not as emotional or risk-adverse as a girl.) There were a few ways that we directed Robby toward good Christian community.

First, we were bold about encouraging men to speak into his life. While we never asked anyone to enter into a relationship with him, when such a relationship naturally occurred, we were supportive and always took time to talk with those men. We would tell them we were grateful for their influence and ask them to continue to speak into Robby's life.

Let me, Dannah, emphasize once more that most of this time was not spent in deep conversation but in simply "being." At different points, men who influenced Robby ran with him, lifted weights with him, did math with him, or ate lethally hot wings with him. There was probably not a lot of talk, but Robby got to be near "good" men, and that rubs off.

Second, we were involved in Robby's selection of his peer community. No parent can truly select a child's friend for them, but you can create opportunities to encourage relationships. We had the Stauffer family over a lot. Not just because we liked them, but because we like Ryan's presence in Robby's life. There were other friendships like this that we helped Robby pursue. I cooked for his friends, and together we achieved a goal we had set before we were married—setting up a great basement hangout for teenagers! We were actively involved in his friendships. In fact, recently, one of Robby's college roommates asked Bob to be his mentor.

Finally, we simply created experiences for larger communities of men to gather around both Robby and me, Bob. Because I believe a man never walks well when he walks alone. So I choose to walk in community with my son and other men of faith. Although Bible studies, men's accountability groups, and more formal gatherings are helpful, I'd like to suggest that some of the more informal community catalysts are important and should not be overlooked. Introducing…fantasy football. Robby's friends and mine join together each year to call it. Don't underestimate the power of competition and fun!

I had some explaining to do when my best friend, Troy VanLiere, named his team the Hooterville Players. (It was a reference to where we went to college…in the middle of a cornfield and so named after the town in the old television series *Green Acres*.) Sadly, a national restaurant chain had taken the innocence right out of it for the younger guys. And *that* is why they need Wolf Dads to walk the path of life with them. Who knows what lurks in the shadows along the way?

The older guys wrinkled their noses at that restaurant chain and made fun of it by saying, "Oh, I hear guys go there *'just for the wings.'* Yeah, right!" I'd like to think that was a teaching moment for my son on the path of his life purpose. He was surrounded by wise men that night.

And they curled their lips and let out a low growl at Hooters. Did the wolf pups in the room understand? I hope they did. The last time I visited a frat house at Penn State it was covered with stickers the guys had brought back from Hooters. I haven't noticed any in Robby's apartment.

That's a "rite of passage" I hope my son chooses never to undergo.

I can already see that Robby is choosing to be encouraged by the community of good men who have been examples for him. It's great to see community working as God intended it.

His Way

Are you allowing your son's dad to be a Wolf Dad? If not, why not? What do you need to change in your heart to be more affirming, or what do you need to do in order to be more patient with an uninvolved dad? Take some time to think through strategies so you can be as supportive as possible. Maybe write down in the margin a list of things you need to do better in your relationship with your son's father. After you do this, take time to write a list of three to five men you currently have walking with your son or whom you desire to see walking with him. Think about how you can facilitate community with those men, and set a few simple goals to get started.

_____

_____

_____

_____

_____

_____

_____

_____

_____

_____

_____

_____

_____

_____

_____

Prayer for purpose and community
based on Proverbs 13:20

Dear Lord, forgive me for the ways I have contributed to emasculating my son's father. Help me to speak words of affirmation in any way that I can; help me step back and support the efforts he does make to father our precious boy. Please, God, give my son and his father a passion to be in community together. And please help my husband (my son's father) to be strong in his leadership in order to demonstrate what a man looks like.

Lord, I believe that he who walks with the wise grows wise but a companion of fools suffers harm. I don't want my son to suffer harm, and I deeply desire for him to be wise. Please help _____ (insert your son's name) to choose wise friends. Today, I feel led to pray for his relationships with _____ (insert the names of friends). I ask that these would be godly friendships or that you'd allow them to fall apart so godly friendships can replace them. And help me to be intentional about helping him find wise mentors so he can walk with them and grow wise. Today, I feel led to pray for his relationships with _____ (insert names of older men in your son's life). Help these men to see how valuable they are to _____ (insert your son's name) and to desire to be good examples for him. In Jesus' Name, amen!

Can you raise a good son without Dad?

I want to speak a gentle word to the mothers who are parenting alone. This is hardly ever by choice. No one ever sets out on the journey of life saying, "Gee, I'd like to be a single mom." But it happens nonetheless. Many moms pick themselves up and succeed in raising great sons. Take, for example, these good men who came out of fatherless homes:

- President George Washington
- John Hancock
- President Thomas Jefferson

- Aristotle
- Nelson Mandela
- Sir Isaac Newton
- Hans Christian Andersen
- Booker T. Washington

The appropriate question isn't "*Can* you raise a son without a dad?" It's "*Should* you?"

The answer is no. Not if you can help it, and if there is any possibility that the marriage can be reconciled. Divorce should never be taken lightly. I have never spoken to a divorced mother who recommends it or is happier because of it.

Social-science data overwhelmingly declares that boys in father-absent homes are more at risk to be poor, become teen "fathers," fail in school, use drugs, be involved in criminal activity…and seek authentic male community in unhealthy places such as gangs. This hardly sets a boy on a trajectory to become a "good" man.

In a fatherless generation, where the picture of manhood is distorted and almost nonexistent, we have a generation of young men crying out for one thing—definition. Definition comes from a father and an extended community of men who initiate our sons into manhood through rite-of-passage experiences. In short: Your son is best taught to direct his natural energies of risk-taking and aggressiveness toward a good purpose by having another man show him how to do it.

If you do not have the blessing of having a man in your life—either a husband or a cooperative father to your children—you can rest assured that the Lord will be a father to your fatherless children. Stay on your knees and believe that he can straighten any crooked road for your children.

"I am a single mother, and my biggest concern has been information on his body and the changes it has gone through and will go through."

Patricia, mother of Zachary, 12

CHAPTER 10

Way #4: Celebrate His Entrance into Manhood

M o-om!" Lexi was about to tattle. I could hear it in her little voice. "There are girls at school who are touching Robby's head and calling him 'Velvet.'" Her tone betrayed her anxiety over the situation. I glanced over at Robby, who just shrugged his shoulders.

Inspired by a youth leader, Robby had recently shaved his sixth-grade head. Now with the hair growing in, it truly did feel like velvet. I loved touching it. But did I want girls his age touching it too? Was Lexi possibly overreacting? I'd find out the next day.

I pulled into the school parking lot to pick up my kids. Robby was there before I knew it and quickly opened the passenger door and plopped

God's Way

"I made a covenant with my eyes not to look lustfully at a girl."

JOB 31:1

CORE VALUE: PURITY

into the front seat. Lexi was lagging, so we waited. Suddenly, the familiar faces of three of Robby's female classmates were at the window of his door, inviting him to roll it down.

They giggled when he did, and one of them coyly said, "Hi, Velvet!"

Another reached in and began stroking his head…in front of me!

Counting to ten as I moved, I opened my door, walked around the minivan, and motioned for the girls to join me a few feet away from Robby. They looked innocently confused at my obvious frustration.

"Girls," I said as lovingly as I could. "You see that velvet over there?"

They smiled, bobbing their heads up and down and saying in unison, "Oh yes!"

"That's *my* velvet," I asserted.

The smiles on their faces fell to the ground.

"Until Robby Gresh is in a marriage relationship, no girl needs to touch him…velvet or no velvet, okay?"

I turned and walked back to my minivan.

I know something about aggressive girls.

My son, sweetly humble in his approach to all of life, is no player. And sometimes girls have taken advantage of that.

(Incidentally, the three "velvet" girls are really sweet friends of his and meant no harm by their touching. But I loved Robby and *them* enough to let them know that going along with the crowd's empty-headed touching and flirting is wrong.)

This chapter will give you some ideas on how to prepare your son for aggressive girls, and his own growing desires in the area of sexuality. Here I take you back to one of the tasks that the "wolfing" picture tells us belongs to the mom (and your e-mails tell

Random Bob Thoughts: That was intense…a little awkward…but definitely a great move!

me comes naturally to you): *safety*. Oh, it might not seem like talking to him about pubic hair and wet dreams is in that category, but it is. Just as you taught him to take a bath, wipe his nose, and wash his hands before he eats so that he would be healthy, so must you and, importantly, his father help him learn how to deal with his body's entrance into manhood. And that means it's time to talk about sex.

Sex and Your Boy's Character

Sex is the topic that you've told me is your greatest fear. Aggressive girls. Porn. Masturbation. Premarital relations. These things all fall into the category of sexual impurity, and they scare a mom silly. But God does not give us a spirit of fear. Instead, he invites us to step up with power, which you get through knowledge and prayer; lots of love, which comes through honest communication; and a sound mind, which is the reward for tackling the topics well.

On a recent *Focus on the Family* broadcast, I heard author and speaker Steve Farrar wrap an entire message to men on sexual integrity around this key thought:

> *Reputation is what people think you are;*
> *Character is who you are when no one is around.*

Since character is the bedrock of a "good" man, I want to dwell on this, as it relates specifically to your son's increasing sexual desires during the older tween years, when his body is becoming that of a man. (It will shock you one day to walk into his bedroom and see a hairy, man-sized leg sticking out of the covers, but never fear...you'll recognize the toes!) In that same bed, your son will face struggles when no one is around and his body is speaking very loudly with desire. It's then that character kicks in to direct his decisions—whether he's a 45-year-old father of four or a 12-year-old who has just had his first wet dream.

Your Son's Changing Body

Inevitably, your son is going to go through a powerful physical change in his body, much like you did when you were a tween or early teenager. Moms often don't realize that this change is as emotionally and physically challenging for a boy as it is for a girl. Since we don't tend to see the signs as easily, we incorrectly conclude that the changes are not as extreme.

We think there are not as many changes in his body that are *visible* (like breast buds), or that directly require *teaching* (like how to care for yourself during your period); and we believe our boys tend to be less *emotional* (no crying, like our daughters may experience when they go through puberty). But all those are myths the female mind embraces due to a lack of knowledge, and that leaves us powerless. Let's muscle up!

Your son's body changes visibly. The first sign is usually pubic hair, followed by his penis growing up to eight times larger than it once was and his scrotum dropping and becoming loose to carefully house his testicles, with all their life-generating sperm. These signs can begin when he is as young as *nine years old*...and while you may not notice, he does!

The process of puberty takes three to four years, and it's not until the latter part of those years that you see the more obvious changes. These include his voice changing—the squeaking can last up to six months—and muscle development. Without even lifting a weight, he will experience rapid change in hormones and neurochemicals that will build muscle and mass in his body. This change marks him as a man, and is lamented when it comes later and he can't hold his own at basketball tryouts in high school.

Your son will experience changes that require teaching him how to care for himself. From wet dreams—God's gentle release for building sexual tension—to a lot of erections, your son is going to experience involuntary bodily occurrences. These require someone to speak frankly to him so that he *knows* he must respond with character. He needs to be taught how to respond to these things, or they can be just as troubling—perhaps more so—as it is to a girl to wake up in bloodied sheets, never having been told about her period.

Singled moms

Should I talk to him about this stuff?

Maybe. Maybe not. Each boy will be different in how comfortable he is discussing sexual issues with his mother. Angela Thomas had this experience:

"I tried to broach the subject with my boys a couple of times and they were like, 'Mom, noooo!' So I went to a neighbor who was a pastor and said, 'You're gonna have to sit 'em down and have the big hoo-ha talk.' They didn't want to receive it from me. There are many boys who are more open to talking about this stuff with their moms. It's a case-by-case decision."

—Angela Thomas

Your son will become highly emotional. He just won't cry. Instead he's most likely to become aggressive, and some boys experience anger or depression. His emotional changes will tend to take place inwardly, as opposed to a girl's outward manifestations of tears and emotional drama.

What's happening in there that's driving all of these changes? Testosterone! We introduced you to the chemical of the Y-chromosome world in an earlier chapter. A boy experiences five to seven strong surges of it throughout the day during puberty. Here's what we didn't tell you. Those surges result in

- erections
- a greater sexual awareness
- a need for more sleep
- clumsiness
- moodiness
- aggressive behavior
- tension in the mother–son relationship

Whoa! Did you catch that last one? Don't be angry with him over the tension. Don't get hurt, but he may shy away from the warm and tactile relationship he once enjoyed with Mom. Just as a girl may become awkward around her dad when her body starts to change, your son is very aware of his physical changes. For example, if you once cuddled with him at bedtime and gave him a gentle back rub, he may become less comfortable with this when testosterone kicks in, for obvious reasons. His body isn't reacting to sexual attraction so much as it's just kind of on overdrive—and who knows when one of those hormone surges will strike next!

This is one reason why we, Bob and Dannah, believe that a dad is so crucial in helping a son celebrate and understand the passage into manhood. Go get your man and ask him to share this chapter with you. The four of us are going to have a heart-to-heart about all things male.

If he's left alone, all of the changes a boy is experiencing in his body can direct him toward some "bad" stuff and away from being morally good. Masturbation, porn, and sexual acting out! These are the years to stake a claim for your son's purity, and it takes a man to draw his heart out to do that. (Mom gets to play the supporting role here.) We believe that dad should talk with him about the issues in this chapter, if at all possible. Here are three ongoing discussions you need to get started with head-on conversations while your son is a tween.

Aggressive Girls

We think the first conversation you should begin is one about aggressive girls. There's one reason we've included the topic of aggressive girls in this chapter: *testosterone*. The topic could go in a few of the upcoming chapters where we'll deal with porn and dating, but it seems like it fits here. Why? Because a young man who's being overwhelmed by his body's new and overactive sexual hormones doesn't need a girl throwing herself at him. Add in spoken and unspoken messages from the culture, and you have a lot of worried moms out there. One mom wrote this on our Secret Keeper Girl blog:

> *My main concern for my son as he becomes a teen is aggressive girls. I want my son to be as virtuous and pure as my*

daughter...but in today's culture it's just as hard—maybe harder—to raise a virtuous boy. I am confident in Jace remaining honest and kind, but less confident in my ability to instill the value of purity in his heart in such a way that he remains pure till his wedding day. I'm afraid that as a teen his peer group and the media's lies will be louder than any of the messages I have instilled. Add to this aggressive girls who make it all too easy for him to follow that path.

Why is this happening more and more? Sadly, the culture has told our daughters that they can and should be the kind of women who go after whatever they think will make them happy. Often the television shows, movies, and songs targeting girl tweens promote empowerment via the control of young men through beauty and sensuality. The girls who swallow these feminist messages of aggression have no idea how delicate the hormonal systems of their male classmates can be! (Translation: We believe that most tween girls have no idea what they're doing when they brush their hand over a middle-school-aged boy's freshly shaven head and sensually call him "Velvet"!)

Here are a few things you can do to help your son be prepared for aggressive girls. (There's more coming up on the conversation about girls, but we're going to stay focused on aggressive girls in this chapter.)

Start talking to him about aggressive girls when he's nine or ten. Yes, he'll probably still think they have "cooties." This is the best time to introduce the topic. It's much easier to have these conversations before the hormones hit.

You may sense that your son, at about the age of nine or ten, is more prone to look at women sexually than he was earlier. I, Dannah, specifically remember a time when I became aware that Robby saw the sexual power—or aggression—of a woman. He was channel-surfing while I was cleaning the house, when he landed for a moment on a mildly sexual video of Britney Spears. She was covered in glitter. Her eyes were made up in dark eyeliner, and her hair was a flawless flaxen mane. She wasn't wearing much, as usual.

My immediate reaction was to take control and grab the remote, but I was caught off guard by the look in Robby's eye. It made me so very sad. After a few moments, he flipped the TV off and looked at me: "Mom, there's something bad about that. It's like she wants to be beautiful but... she's not." His sweet innocence was aware that, though he *wanted* to look, he shouldn't. I'm fairly sure he wasn't even nine.

Use teachable moments to help him see that not all girls are the same. We think that the time to begin helping him distinguish between good girls and aggressive girls is when he's just beginning to notice a difference. When he's nine or ten you may not even be talking with him about a wife or dating, but it's important to begin to help him see the difference between an aggressive girl and a good girl.

When you find yourself in a teachable moment, like I did with that Britney Spears video, take a moment to say something like, "Not all girls are the same. Some are good, and some are what I'd call aggressive. The Bible has something to say about them, and it is not good. Sometime I'd like to share that with you."

Few boys are going to run into Britney Spears in real life. But you can use his first notice of the Victoria's Secret poster or Hooters billboard to prepare him for girls who emulate the behavior promoted by such celebrities and brands.

Show him that God says to stay away from aggressive girls. In another day, Proverbs 7 might not have been nearly as much needed for every boy. But today it is. Follow up the brief conversation you began in his teachable moment by opening the Bible to read Proverbs 7 together. Don't get too overwhelmed by the whole chapter, but focus on key verses, such as where it says a boy who looks too long at a girl like that "lacks sense" (verse 7). Another good one to focus on is this: "Do not let your heart turn aside to her ways, do not stray into her paths" (verse 25 NKJV). In other words—"Stay away!"

Of course, you don't want him to stay away from girls altogether. In fact, pointing out and talking well of godly young women is one of the best ways to help him safeguard his heart and his purity (We'll explore healthy guy–girl relationships in chapter 12.) One day you want him to find someone who is as good as he is. And you'll hope they have grand-babies to bring home to you. That means you'll need to introduce to him the idea of how to make grand-babies. The next conversation to begin is the one about S-E-X!

Sex

We've believed for a very long time—because wiser Christian counselors than ourselves with big fat degrees behind their names have said so—that it's critical to talk to your children about sex at about the age of ten. Since we've already demonstrated in an earlier chapter that moral values are formed during the critical tween years, it's critical that you begin a conversation with them about sex during those same years.

Of course, every child develops at a different rate both physically and emotionally. There will be excep-tions. But consider this: It's much easier to build a sexual value system by introducing the concept to them yourselves than it is to dismantle a faulty one built by friends, television—or worse yet, porn. It's a strate-gic choice to introduce words like *penis* and *intercourse* before everyone else does. Because of the time and culture we are living in, talk to him no later than his tenth or eleventh year. Here are a few tips to make it a little easier to form the words.

> ### The questions
>
> "How far is too far?"
>
> "How will I know if she's 'the one'?"
>
> "Why is porn bad?"
>
> "What if I like guys?"
>
> "Can I masturbate if I'm not looking at porn?"
>
> Do you know the answer to these questions? They're the ones you'll need to help your son answer during his teen years. They will inform his sexual theology and world-view. Some of our other books, like *And the Bride Wore White, Who Moved the Goal-post?*, and more recently *What Are You Waiting For?* address these tough questions.

Whatever his age, be prepared to answer any questions truthfully. The good news is, if your son is ready to hear about the basic mechanics of sex, he often asks. Lexi brought the topic up with me, Dannah, when she was five. She didn't get the whole sex-education lesson then, but we did begin talking.

Robby didn't bring up the topic of sex before we did, but after the first conversation he would ask questions that we needed to address with truth. For example, once our family stopped at a gas station on a vacation. Having just seen a vending machine in the men's room, he bounced up beside me and happily asked, "Mom, what's a condom?" I'm sad to say that I choked—but Bob was calm, cool, and collected. Since the question was asked in front of his little sister, who'd already had her initial conversation about sex, they both got the answer. He simply said, "That's a small piece of latex that a man might put on his penis before he has sex with a woman so they won't get pregnant."

"Awkward!" said Lexi as she giggled.

"Sorry I asked," said Robby.

And our family rolled on with the certainty that Dad, if not Mom, knew all the answers in the universe about anything sexual. And that's why you answer tough questions when they are young...so they think you have the answers when they are older and their brains begin to wrestle with much more critical worldview questions about sex. Like, is contraception good or bad? What harm can porn do? Is it okay to be gay? How far is too far? Do I have to get married to have sex, because not all Bible charac-ters did? You want to inform their values more than you want to inform them of the mechanics!

Random Bob Thought: Very awkward!

Be accurate and explicit in conversations you initiate. At some point, you'll need to set aside some time for an initial conversation, hopefully before your child is ten. (Even if your child asks a question that prompts the big talk, it's easy to say, "Let's talk about that tonight when we're home alone. I want to take some time to answer your question carefully because it's a really important one." That's what I did with Lexi.)

Robby never asked, so we had to initiate, and we did this intentionally a few days before his tenth birthday. In *Six Ways to Keep the "Little" in Your Girl*, I, Dannah, shared the conversation I overheard Bob have with Robby. It went something like this:

> Bob: *Robby, I want to tell you about sex. Do you know about sex?*
>
> Robby: *Yes. I do.*
>
> (Our hearts were beating wildly at this point, thinking we'd missed it. Someone else had told him, and I had so wanted it to be Bob!)
>
> Bob: *Where did you learn about it?*
>
> Robby: *On the Internet.*
>
> Bob: *What do you mean by that?*
>
> Robby: *Well, sometimes when I play games on the Internet it says, "Sex: male or female?" So I know about that, Dad.*
>
> Bob: *Well, that's how the word sex is used as a noun. I'm going to tell you how it's used as a verb.*

I, Bob, really want to urge you dads to step up and have the conversation father to son. You made the kid. You know how it works. Now it's time to tell him. I'm assuming you could figure it out, but just in case:

> *Sex is a really great gift that God gave to a husband and wife to show their love to each other and to create babies. Have you ever wondered how a baby gets into a woman's belly? Well, God said it was okay for a husband and wife to be naked together because God put sperm inside the penis of a man. This has to get into the private part of a woman called the vagina, where she has an egg. If the sperm can*

get to the egg it can become a baby. So, when the husband and wife are hugging each other and naked, sometimes the man will put his penis into her vagina hoping they can have a baby.

Pretty basic, right? Well, that's all they need when they are first hearing about it: the basic mechanics and a good solid assurance that it's approved by God within the confines of marriage.

This conversation may lead to a lot of questions. Some kids laugh. Others think it's kind of gross. Still others are fascinated enough to ask a lot of questions, and guess what? You *get* to answer them. How you respond to those questions is as important as introducing the basics.

Be positive. I, Bob, have certainly had my share of sexual sin, which mars my ability to see the beauty of God's gift through my own eyes of shame. As I told you in the introduction to this book, although I was a virgin when I married Dannah, my eyes and my heart were not pure. Many men struggle with the same sense of shame, or have a continuing struggle to have pure minds and hearts. You can't let that be an excuse to not speak about sex with your son—and please don't be negative about the gift because of your falling short. If you choose that route—to be silent based on your fear—you create a place of isolation for your son to face his own temptations.

For a connecting mom's (and dad's) toolbox

Being fully healed from sin in your past is what enables you to speak positively to your children about God's gift of sex. Here are a few of our favorite resources to help you:

- *Pursuing the Pearl: The Quest for a Pure, Passionate Marriage* by Dannah Gresh is great for moms if you've got some sexual sin in your past and you're looking for healing.

- *Samson and the Pirate Monks* by Nate Larkin is great for dads and will deal with issues of past sexual sin and current temptation by calling you into authentic community with other men.

And that's what plants and waters shame. Dad, you've got to speak up and be positive.

Filling our kids with negative "don't-have-sex" messages is using a strategy of fear. God does not give us a spirit of fear. So, your approach isn't of him if it's full of warnings, dire predictions, and a chorus of "don'ts." When temptation arises, your son will end up turning elsewhere for advice—if he turns anywhere—so stay positive. The only way I know to do that is to deal with your own junk. Dannah and I both had a lot of hurt and sin in our past to deal with, but we were able to use our healing as a foundation for a positive approach to sex education in our home.

Remember, this big talk is only the beginning. For the next 10 to 12 years you'll be helping him build a sexual value system. He's going to decide what his theology about sex is and what he believes about marriage and family, and he's going to fight—or not fight—a battle for purity. If you want the honor of being in the fight with him, present sex and marriage as a beautiful picture of Christ and the church. There's so much good stuff to share.

One of the good things you can share with him is the wonder of how God created his body to form life. That means you've got to talk about something good that's capable of a lot of bad if it's not coupled with character. Yes, we're going to have to talk about his penis.

The Body Part You Don't Have

Boys like their penises. This is a fact. I, Dannah, was once at a women's retreat where young mothers suddenly began talking about all the experiences they'd had with their preschool boys and their penises. Shameless in the wonder of it all, these boys would say and do the darnedest things. From claiming it was a "hose" they could use to clean off their sky fort to hanging Christmas ornaments off them with great pride, I heard some pretty unusual stories that night. We all concluded as moms that we shouldn't make too much of it. Boys will be boys. And they all have one of *those*!

But during the tween years, it's time to begin to direct the fascination toward a holy calling to one wife! It's time to begin to teach your son to respond to his fascination and desires with godly Christian *character*. This is best done through a conversation with Dad, who can assure the boy he's been there experiencing all the new beginnings. Such as more noticeable erections—your son has been having them since he was a baby, but remember that his penis is about to undergo prolific growth. Such as suddenly waking up in the middle of a wet dream. A guy understandably will have some questions that need to be answered.

Allow me, Bob, to step in to this rather explicit conversation. In fact, this is probably a conversation meant to be between father and father, but we'll let you moms stay in the room for the sake of knowing what in the world is going on. Here are the first two things a dad needs to cover when his son is hitting puberty.

Tell him what to do with an erection! We know that must sound strange, but without some instruction there's one obvious option: masturbate. Since a boy may be experiencing an erection several times a day, he may also be making a decision about masturbation several times a day. While many scholars—both biblical and secular—say, "Have at it," we don't agree, even though there is nowhere in Scripture that this topic is directly mentioned. Here's why we suggest that your advice be that he do his best to avoid masturbation as his natural response:

1. First, God created all of our sexual desires to bring us into a one man–one woman relationship. Masturbation is a solo sport, and misuses the desire.

2. Second, masturbation focuses on a selfish desire, rather than a giving of oneself as encouraged in 1 Corinthians 7.

3. Finally, masturbation can lead to addictive habits that include excessive masturbating, porn use, or a fantasy life that's not healthy.

Many argue with us, telling us that masturbation is normal. One publication stated what most do: "Boys may masturbate several times a day, once a month, or not at all. It is a natural way to explore your body and is entirely normal."[1] We would like to argue that a lot of things are "normal" responses, but humanity tends to self-regulate behaviors that don't offer good to society by letting character override the desire.

For example, it's "normal" to want to scream at your kids when they are fussy toddlers, but not good. It's "normal" for a tween boy to want to hit something when he's mad, but not good. It's "normal" for a married man to want to have sex with an attractive but strange woman who dresses immodestly and flirts with him, but it's not good. It's "normal" for any warm-blooded man to want to study the *Sports Illustrated* swimsuit issue, but it's not good. We must plant the quality of *good* (as opposed to "normal") in our son's value system to help him to make the best choices about his behavior. While we strongly encourage you not to be too black-and-white about the issue—creating excessive shame about masturbating, since we do believe it will happen—it is good to set a standard of restraint in this area of a boy's development.

Tell him that wet dreams are a heroic symbol of his purity. All boys will experience wet dreams. An erection happens at night when hormones are surging. While a boy may dream during the erection caused by this surge—it could be romantic or sexual but not necessarily—he usually doesn't masturbate. The body ejaculates naturally. It's involuntary, and a boy should know to expect it or he may be frustrated and insecure when it happens. In most cases wet dreams start when a boy is 12, 13, or 14, but they can happen at a younger age, so it's good to have the conversation early. A boy who is not masturbating and thus is getting no release through self-gratification is likely to experience more wet dreams. Help him to understand that this is good, and a sign of his purity.

The topic of his body and his purity is one you'll want Dad or a father figure in his life to revisit often. It will be on your son's mind continually, and there will be new questions that surface every day. Set yourselves up as the experts, and be ready to answer any question that comes your way. Swallowing your own embarrassment and being honest will be well worth it on his wedding day!

His Way

All right, it's time to make a game plan! Taking into account your son's age and readiness, take a few moments to write down a strategy for discussing issues of purity with him. Set some goals for what you believe you need to discuss with him and what you believe his father should discuss with him. Schedule a time to intentionally discuss this with your man if he hasn't been reading along with you.

_____

_____

_____

_____

_____

_____

_____

_____

_____

_____

_____

_____

_____

_____

Prayer based on Job 31:1

Oh, Lord! We live in a pornographic culture filled with so much sin. I plead with you to protect my son's purity by first protecting his eyes. Lord, would you give my husband (or the name of a father figure in your son's life) a heart desire to covenant with my son that their eyes would not look lustfully at a girl? My desire is that my son would not walk alone in this world of temptation but would have a godly man to walk with him.

Please make my husband (or the name of a father figure in your son's life) a man of sexual integrity my son can talk to through his teen years. Give us wisdom to know when to talk about these things, and when to let him come to us. I ask you to break any cycle of sexual sin in our family. Let sexual integrity mark my son's life. I pray for this in the Name of Jesus, amen.

"Pornography scares my mommy heart to pieces. It seems that the world wants to steal my little boy away using this powerful drug. We have put protection on our computers, limit what video games and movies he can watch, and are careful about what reading materials enter our home, and yet the predator is still out there. Even as our 13-year-old walks through the mall he is assaulted by images of women...it is everywhere."

Tracey, mother of Samuel, 13

CHAPTER 11

Way #5: Unplug Him from a Plugged-In World

"Click here for T&A."

I was helping my ten-year-old son work from a website that contained codes for his PlayStation game, when I was confronted with it. It was there just throbbing, waiting for a young unsupervised kid to follow its trail.

Surely that's not what I think it is, I thought to myself, determined to find out.

A few moments later, armed with the codes that would save his virtual world, my son hopped off the desk chair and I hopped on.

Click.

But it was as I feared. There she was. A brunette, wearing nothing but a thong and a wet T-shirt, rolled in the sand

God's Way

"I will walk within my house in the integrity of my heart. I will set no worthless thing before my eyes…A perverse heart shall depart from me; I will know no evil."

Psalm 101:2-4 NASB

Core Values: Honor, RESPONSIBILITY

of a sun-kissed beach. Her pose enhanced every barely hidden curve. Aroused nipples pushed through her white T-shirt. Her eyes said more than words ever could.

Softcore porn.

The kind that makes the *Sports Illustrated* swimsuit issue every man's temptation.

And my son was one click away from it.

Twenty-five percent of children as young as 10 unintentionally encounter sexual content on the Internet.[1] But the sadder fact is, there are a lot of kids that young who seek it out. Roughly 42 percent of kids aged 10 to 17 have viewed porn in the last 12 months.[2] For many of our sons, this will start a lifelong battle that some will never win, with careers, marriages, and children destroyed in the aftermath of an addiction that's becoming commonplace.

In Our Culture, Porn Is "Normal"

One of the greatest struggles for your son's goodness will be staged on the playing field of porn. It's come out of dark and dusty adult stores to fill our everyday lives. It's pretty scary, isn't it? In the last ten years porn stars have become mainstream celebrities. Where once their names were only known in the sordid circle of the sin itself, our culture now celebrates women like Jenna Jameson, who wrote a bestselling book entitled *How to Make Love Like a Porn Star.* Television networks host programs like *The Girls Next Door*, filmed in the Playboy Mansion and featuring Playboy bunnies like Holly Madison and Kendra Wilkinson, whose names are now familiar to us. Need a little homosexual fuel for your fantasy life? Try RuPaul's *Drag Race*, a reality show that features homosexual men in a competition to be the next famous drag queen.

These kinds of things—whether we allow them into our homes or not—normalize porn. Before we realized it, even prime-time television was filled with sexual display that was unthinkable only a couple of decades ago. As a culture our senses have become numb to blatant sexuality because it is so pervasive. We don't even think twice anymore when we walk by a five-story billboard of a barely clad lingerie model.

And the Internet is readily available to feed progressively more perverted sexual scenarios and fantasies to our sons. I want you to know that what your kids could see via the Internet makes *Playboy* and *Penthouse* look like kids' stuff. Psychologist Dr. Linda Papadopoulos researched the impact looking at porn had on teenagers. One startling revelation was that girls were beginning to feel uncomfortable that their boyfriends were behaving violently or asking them to do strange sexual acts. She warned,

> *This isn't the type of pornography that was around when we were teenagers. What kids are seeing today is very often violent, and it has no intimacy, no respect, no kindness, no context of sex within a loving relationship. It is very damaging to young people and their relationships.*[3]

Make no mistake about it, today's porn doesn't just misuse God's gift of sexuality—it misrepresents it grotesquely. The explicit, often dominating, self-serving porn your son could stumble onto through the Internet has the power to completely dismantle his esteem for the loving, tender relationship God wants him to know within marriage. Let's look at some proactive ways to protect him from this modern-day evil.

Filter Him

Every family with Internet access in the home should have a filtering system in place to protect the whole family. Can I ask you a question? Let's say you walk into your house and find a copy of *Hustler*, considered to contain some of the more explicit magazine porn available, as well as copies of *Playboy* and *Penthouse* sitting on your coffee table. Would you simply cover them up with your *Good Housekeeping* and *Time* magazines? Of course not, but that's what many families do every single day when they fail to protect their families from the access to porn through the Internet.

There are many great filters available today for your online and handheld devices. (Even the iPad has filtering software!) The ones we use in our home are Safe Eyes and Covenant Eyes.

Safe Eyes is an actual filter. It gives you control to block websites, specific kinds of web content, and online movies and TV, and it will even help you monitor Facebook and other social media. We like the feature that controls the hours per day of screen time and enables us to block web usage after any time of day we choose. (Our web curfew is 10:30 at night.) This kind of software is easily downloaded and enables you to actually control what you and your children can view. Learn more about Safe Eyes at internetsafety.com.

Covenant Eyes is an accountability program. When you subscribe, you give the e-mail addresses of accountability partners to the service. Those accountability partners—they could be you or your husband's accountability partner—receive a regular report on every single website that has been visited during the report period. Inappropriate content is red-flagged. This kind of software is great for older children because it allows them to learn to navigate making decisions to say "no" to porn, violence, and obscene language. (They won't always be under our watchful eye. It's important to teach them to make good choices when they are about to leave the nest!) Learn more about this accountability software at covenanteyes.com.

Click here!

Before you give your son a smart phone or even an iTouch, make sure you have taken time to get online and research how you can block porn from his device. While all of the major phone carriers offer some type of blocking, most of these services are easily overridden. You need to be able to block porn from the device itself. And not all of them are created equally. We've found that Apple products (iPhone, iTouch, iPad, and so on) are far easier to control than others. Do your own research, but make your son's purity a major factor when you decide what device you might hand to him.

Filters in place? Don't breath too easy! We're hearing more and more reports about kids getting into trouble with porn at a friend's house…or even in their classrooms at school.

Singled moms

How do I talk to my son about porn?

"Porn was easier for me to talk to my sons about than their changing bodies. I still asked godly men in their lives to speak to them. But I also said, 'There are inappropriate things you can't see.' I was not descriptive. Then I taught them to filter. Our TV has a mechanism that blocks inappropriate material. I have to punch in a code to let them view things. When they go to a movie, I tell them, 'You have a filter—a biblical filter in your heart. If you get in a movie and it is inappropriate, I need you to walk out.'

"My boys have old-school cell phones with calling and texting only. No photos and no Internet access. A lot of the boys with access to the Internet on their phones are going into their bedrooms and viewing pornography! Because we have been having these conversations for years since they were very small, both of my boys say, 'You're right, Mom! You're right!'"

—Angela Thomas

Train Him

You can't just block your son from porn. You have to train him to choose to block himself! Otherwise, he *will* be vulnerable to the predatory industry that out-profits NASCAR, the National Football League, the National Hockey League, basketball, and baseball *combined*. Yes, you read that correctly. The profits from all five of those very lucrative sports industries together don't equal the profit made in the porn industry in our nation alone. While Hollywood brings us about 300 movies a year, the porn industry releases about 700...per month!

My point is this: The porn industry didn't get that way by humbly waiting for patrons to seek it out. It got that way preying upon our grandfathers, husbands, sons—and one day our grandsons will be the targets. You can't just hide your son from porn. You have to train him to say "no" to it.

Talk to him about pornography beginning about the age of seven or eight. Gee, that sounds so soon. But in 2009, "sex" was the fourth most searched word on the Internet for children aged 8 to 12.[4] It's curiosity that drives them there, but sadly this curiosity is dropping the median age of first exposure year after year. More recently we've read different studies that pinpoint a boy's first exposure to as young as nine. If you don't begin to equip him to fight against porn at a young age, his mind and heart will be susceptible to its siren call the first time he is exposed.

You don't need to explain the details of what porn is when he's this young, but you do need to give him messages that keep him alert to the fact that you know about it and that it's bad. You might simply explain that looking at pornography means you are looking at pictures of naked or almost naked people and we're not supposed to do that. A boy at that age doesn't really have the chemicals to attract him to such a thing and will likely think it sounds "gross." Key to this conversation is communicating the unmistakable understanding that porn is bad. Here's a conversation that founder of Men's Leadership Ministries, Steve Farrar, had with his son John:

> Steve: *"Have you ever been real thirsty?"*
>
> John: *"Oh yeah, Dad. I've been real thirsty."*
>
> Steve: *"Have ya ever been...I mean really thirsty, John?"*
>
> John: *"Yeah."*
>
> Steve: *"Can you imagine being in a desert and dying of thirst?"*
>
> John: *"Okay—yeah?"*
>
> Steve: *"John, could you ever imagine being so thirsty that you'd find an old abandoned gas station and the only water there was water in an old corroded toilet and you'd drink that water?"*
>
> John: *"Dad, that's gross!"*
>
> Steve: *"I know it's gross. Let me tell you something, man, pornography is toilet water. Pornography is sewer water and you want to keep your mind crystal clear!"*[5]

His son was seven years old when Steve had that conversation with him.

The conversation about pornography will be an ongoing one with your son into his adult years, but begin it when he's young—before he's exposed.

Let him know that he's not alone. This is where Dad or a father figure becomes really important. Pornography is every man's battle. (Strong statement? We don't think so. Even a godly man who has never clicked a porn link on the Internet has to walk past the Victoria's Secret posters in the mall.) No boy should feel the sense of shameful isolation that comes from believing the lie that he's all alone in this battle. The Christian community, though it's come a long way, can create that illusion. Author Ed Young writes,

> *Based on what is depicted by the media, any alien visitor to America would likely conclude that every person over the age of twelve is sexually active, that marriage is the last place to look for sexual satisfaction, that faithfulness is a nostalgic dream, and that even the sickest of perversions is nothing less than every citizen's "inalienable right."*
>
> *This would be true, of course, unless they happened to visit the church. Then they would probably wonder whatever became of sex. They might never hear it mentioned at all— or perhaps only spoken of in whispers or condemning tones. Historically, to its shame, the church has either ignored the God-given gift of human sexuality or smothered it in an avalanche of "thou-shalt-nots."*[6]

Don't let that be true of your church if you can be a part of solving the problem. But if you can't fix it there, make sure your children feel like home is a safe and open place to discuss sexuality with you.

At key points in Robby's life, both Dannah and I sat down to share with him our failures and God's incredible redemption in our lives. Dannah did this with Robby when he was about 14, and I did it almost regularly as we sought to build a sense in him that if he falls, we can handle it, and we're here to help him heal. We were never graphic, and because we had both achieved a lot of healing we were able to maintain our roles as leaders and parents. (In other words, we weren't tempted to try to heal through making a confession to him.) We were very age-appropriate. We also sent a strong message that we hoped he wouldn't fall and that by God's grace he could live in purity. But we were honest.

A lot of parents are afraid of these kinds of conversations. You should be more afraid of *not* having them. Satan uses isolation and shame to fuel a man's hunger for the false intimacy that pornography promises. Don't let your son buy into that lie.

A dad can share—appropriately—what his battle has looked like and how he's winning. He can tell his son that he's not alone, and he can become a safe place where his son will come for shelter when he feels tempted or falls prey to porn.

Screen Him

I am tempted to focus solely on Internet use in this chapter, but I realize that television, cell phones, iPods, and other technology also whisk our boys away from reality into a world that's often unsafe. Overall, the average boy will absorb 38 hours a week of video games, computer time, music, television, and radio.[7] One of the obvious problems with being so plugged in is this: If your son is glued to a screen for 38 hours a week and, as most do, attends a public or private school, how much time does that leave for you to interact with him to form a value system that directs him toward "good"?

Now, most of us know we don't want our sons listening to Eminem rapping out lyrics about which "Spice Girl I wanna impregnate." We're really hoping they don't sneak a peek at HBO's *G-String Diva* reruns while we're in the shower at a hotel. Wise parents will always keep an eye and ear bent toward what their kids are seeing and hearing in the media. While blatant trash is, well, blatant trash, that's not the only problem.

It's not just the "bad" media that rob our sons of their ability to be "good." (Remember, a prerequisite of being "good" is that your son is wired and programmed to consider the needs of others—to think outside of his own desires and be useful to his family and community.) It's the fact that sitting in front of a screen is becoming an addiction in and of itself. We've seen this with gaming. A screen is the ultimate distraction.

And new research is demonstrating that, as a whole, all this screen use is having a harmful effect on the ability of our brains to connect to others. Specifically, a book entitled *iBrain: Surviving the Technological Alteration of the Modern Mind* argues that too much screen use is decreasing our ability to empathize with others and is leading to an inability to read facial language.[8] Obsessive screen use leads us away from— rather than toward—understanding the needs of other people.

Does that mean we should all move to the country and live like the Amish? Nah. (I tried that one weekend with Bob who has some Amish friends. He went fishing all day and I turned stinky, dirty laundry in a hand washer for four hours. That's not for me!) But we do think there are some things you can do to make your son's screen habits healthier.

> ### What should come before screen time?
>
> When you evaluate how much screen time you'll allot for your son, consider the things that need to be prioritized as of greater value. What should come first? How about…
>
> - quiet time with God
> - Mom time
> - Dad time
> - sibling time
> - chore time
> - school time
> - real playtime outdoors
> - personal care time (boys will never put this first!)
> - sleep time (remember, he needs a lot!)

Turn off screens when you are eating. Mealtimes together have been mentioned a few times in this book. And we want to harp on it one more time! Having dinner as a family has proven to increase kids' academic success and reduce at-risk behavior. Meals create an opportunity to unravel the day's events and advise your kids. Protect the intimacy of conversation at mealtimes. Not sure how to get things rolling? Try a game I've played with my kids called "Hi and Low." Each person gets to share the "high" moment of their day and the "low" moment. It opens their hearts and gives us key information about what's going on in their heads and why they are behaving the way that they are.

Set a good example by being physically active and limiting screen time. Bob and I try to put ourselves under the same limits our kids have. We cannot tell them they can't be screen addicts, when we are addicts ourselves. Our actions speak louder than our words.

As I write this, I'm failing at it. I'm a Facebook and iPhone addict. I tend to always have a screen near me. I need to work on this. That's my next big change. (And I will do it. When I wrote *Six Ways to Keep the "Little" in Your Girl*, God spoke to my heart about the screen usage in our home. I talked to Bob about it, and his heart was in alignment with mine. The Gresh family had lost their intimacy together to screen obsessions. Since we were in the process of moving, we decided to wait until we moved to make our changes more gently. We just never hooked up cable at the new house. And it's awesome.)

I'm in a place right now where I could use a full "screen fast." While I can't be entirely irresponsible and ignore my work, I recently set up some crazy limitations to get myself back in line. I need to be more present, and that—for me—requires some drastic action. I'm pretty sure I will survive without that Facebook post or the late-breaking news in my e-mail box!

What about you? Do you need to consider your own limits as you build some for your son? I meet moms every day who are a little too glued to the Net. (Sadly, this is more true of stay-at-home and home-schooling moms, whose hearts are really in the right place...but sometimes their noses are not! We learned this doing research for one of our projects. We're not pointing any fingers—just reporting what you told us about yourselves.) The sword cuts both ways: I think we serve our children best when we change our own lives.

The bottom line about being plugged in too much is that it disables our ability to pursue our responsibilities with excellence and to be women of honor. And it does the same thing to our husbands and sons if we aren't careful.

Psalm 101:2-4 says, "I will walk within my house in the integrity of my heart. I will set no worthless thing before my eyes…A perverse heart shall depart from me; I will know no evil" (NASB). Worthlessness is what we've got to slay to win the war on porn, slothfulness, and irresponsibility in our son's lives…and our own. Here are some worthless things I looked at today:

- a photo of the Muppets on meth and cookies
- an impressive Facebook post where my girlfriend reported that she got $36.00 worth of groceries for $14.35
- a stress post where a girlfriend lamented her long to-do list
- a victory post where a co-worker announced that his e-mail in-box was empty

Need I go on?

My heart's desire is not to take the fun out of life. Bob and I have enjoyed posting the chase for our runaway peacock, King Tut. (Someone—we don't know who—has even created a King Tut page on Facebook, and it's been hilarious. That roadrunner-of-a-getaway-artist has been writing books, creating TV reality shows, and encouraging our peahen, Cleo, to run away with him.) It's good to have fun. It's good to be connected.

But it's all too easy to cross the line from "having fun" to "worthless," where we become consumed by things that don't really matter much. How many of us have been on YouTube or Facebook, only to look up hours later realizing we have done so at the expense of our relationships and responsibilities? And once we open our hearts to that which is worthless, it's only one small step further into perversity.

> Guard your heart above all else, for it
> determines the course of your life.
>
> Proverbs 4:23 NLT

His Way

Be extra prayerful as you approach the creative process for building a plan to unplug your son from the assault of porn. It's one of the most insidious battles he will face. No mother wants her son to face it, but the reality is that all of them will. Two specific things you can do are 1) determine what filtering you'll do as a family to protect all of you, and 2) determine how and when you will discuss the topic of pornography with him. Take a little time to write down your goals for the next few weeks in the space below.

_____

_____

_____

_____

_____

_____

_____

_____

_____

_____

_____

_____

_____

Prayer based on Psalm 101:2-4

Oh Lord, it is becoming harder and harder to walk within our homes in integrity of heart. Filth of all kinds has made its way in. Please reveal to me any place where my home has become impure because of what is leaking in through computers, cell phones, television, music, movies, books and magazines, or some other means. Let our family be in agreement that we will set no worthless things before our eyes. I specifically pray first for my husband, _____, (or for the father figure in my son's life, _____,) and I ask you to make him a man of integrity to lead my son. And I pray for my son(s), _____. Please let all perverseness depart from them. And let them know no evil. In the Name of Jesus I pray this, amen.

The teen brain: Use it or lose it!

Recent studies produced major advances in understanding how the teenage brain develops. Researchers found that through about age 11 in girls and age 12 in boys, the brain's gray matter is thickening. The brain cells are developing extra connections. After that point, "the gray matter thins as the excess connections are eliminated or pruned," says Dr. Jay Giedd, Chief of Brain Imaging at the Child Psychiatry Branch of NIMH. He continues:

But the pruning-down phase is perhaps even more interesting, because our leading hypothesis for that is the "use it or lose it" principle. Those cells and connections that are used will survive and flourish. Those cells and connections that are not used will wither and die. So if a teen is doing music or sports or academics, those are the cells and connections that will be hard-wired. If they're lying on the couch or playing video games or [watching] MTV, those are the cells and connections that are going [to] survive.[9]

"The biggest challenge is teaching him to be a gentleman, when so many in our society and even in the church culture believe that having him open doors for girls and ladies and simply showing respect for women is 'old-fashioned.' This goes right into my fear: that we teach him one way, but there are so many more loud voices 'out there' (even among believers) that tell him we are outdated and there is a better way. I pray he doesn't buy into Satan's lies."

Xiomara, mother of Jesse, 10

CHAPTER 12

Way #6: Let Him Open the Car Door for You

Lexi was recently watching *Funny Girl*, starring Barbra Streisand. (She's an old soul, my Lexi. She loves recordings of black-and-whites and old musicals and wears them out!) In one scene, the charming and handsome Nick Arnstein is romancing Streisand's Fanny Brice. He is tender, but direct. Clearly, he is leading this relationship and unafraid to pursue her. He touches her with confidence and gazes into her eyes when he speaks to her. When she is shy, he is strong.

"I wish men were like that," said my 17-year-old baby girl.

"Like what?" I asked.

"Like that!" she proclaimed, pointing at the TV screen. "Strong! Unafraid!"

"He's pursuing her like a gentleman. He wants her," I agreed.

God's Way

"Mark this: There will be terrible times in the last days. People will be lovers of themselves…disobedient to their parents… without love…not lovers of the good…lovers of pleasure rather than lovers of God—having a form of godliness but denying its power. Have nothing to do with such people."

2 TIMOTHY 3:1-5

CORE VALUES: FAMILY LOVE, RESPECT

"Yes!" said Lexi, understanding that I got it.

Yes.

Lexi's grown up in an age where television depicts men as crude and stupid. Uninterested in real relationships, but eager to use a woman's body. This lovely old-fashioned taste of romance was winsome and magnetic to both of us. What she saw was a clean-cut man wearing a beautiful tux and behaving like a gentleman. Sadly, the example of Nick Arnstein eventually breaks down because he can't keep his hands off gambling chips and other women, but for a brief moment Lexi and I saw what every girl wants.

A gentleman.

My girl is not alone. In 2006, *Boys Adrift* author Leonard Sax delivered a commencement address at Avon Old Farms, a boy's school in Connecticut. Surprisingly, there were more girls in the audience than boys. Sax inquired why and discovered that the girls were from a nearby private co-ed school, Westminster Academy, and were friends of the boys who were graduating. He approached a group of them after the ceremony because he wanted to know why the girls were here with these boys when they had plenty to pick from at their own school:

> One girl rolled her eyes. "The boys at our school are all such total losers," she said. "Being around them is like being around my younger brother. They're loud and obnoxious and annoying. And they think they're so tough. It's totally nauseating." The other girls laughed and nodded their heads in agreement.

> "And the boys here are really that different?" [Sax] asked.

> They all nodded their heads again. "Totally," another girl said. "The boys here are like—gentlemen. I know that sounds really strange and weird and old-fashioned, but that's just the way it is. Like, they stand up when you come in the room. They open doors for you."[1]

Later, Sax inquired of the headmaster, who said,

It's not enough for the boy to become a man. We want him to become a gentleman.[2]

This expensive, private, boys-only boarding school is turning out gentlemen, and the girls love it! As I was writing this chapter, one mom I surveyed commented,

> *My biggest challenge at this point is to raise little gentle-men. I believe it is very important for them to learn to show respect this way, by opening doors, offering help, and putting others first, but it is so opposite of what the world teaches that we are constantly re-teaching and explaining why "me first" is not God's way.*

That's really the crux of the issue, isn't it? We live in a "me first" world that trains our boys to be the antithesis of what God crafted them to be. Today's boys are told by our culture and by strident feminism that they *are* wimpy and passive and selfish. Instead of being spurred to be disciplined men of honor and integrity, they're told that their bodies are in need of sexual feasting and a whole lot of farting. Instead of being inspired to work to earn the heart of a girl, they are judged by the number of "conquests" they can achieve. So they wholeheartedly embrace their video games, athletics, and porn in a hyperindividualistic approach to life. Why should they rise above mediocrity and selfishness, when they are told that it's their nature as men?

Instead of following the pattern of today's emasculated, me-centered manhood, what if we built sons who rose up to be gentlemen in pursuit of family love? Ladies, let's build some gentlemen!

Family First

I think that the apostle Paul was writing to a culture a lot like ours—and that moms faced a similar battle—when he penned his second letter to Timothy. Verses 1 through 5 in chapter 3 warn,

> *Mark this: There will be terrible times in the last days. People will be lovers of themselves...disobedient to their parents... without love...not lovers of the good...lovers of pleasure*

rather than lovers of God—having a form of godliness but denying its power. Have nothing to do with such people.

This sounds all too much like the "me culture" our society has created. Self-centered. Not caring to do good. Desiring pleasure. In essence, Paul was describing the apathetic "bad boy" mentality we are experiencing today.

Let me show you something that'll blow your mind. The phrase "without love" in 2 Timothy is the translation of the original Greek word *astorgos*. *Astorgos* referred to the lack of a certain kind of love, though. Not just any kind. Specifically, Paul was saying that in the last days there will be people who are "without *family* love."

Fatherless.

Disobedient.

Selfish.

On their own.

Not caring for the needs of others.

Sounds like us! I believe that the root of our "me first" culture is a lack of family love. I want to challenge you to *reclaim* family love by building in your son a desire to be a husband and a father, and the courage to be the kind of man that makes a woman feel *wanted*! Let me suggest that you'll do this best by teaching him to be a gentleman.

A Better-Than-Rubies Wife

Our boys have a great need to have a holy desire to search for a wife of great worth. Proverbs 31 declares that an excellent wife is better than rubies. Did you know that a ruby is far more valuable than a diamond? They are among the most precious of earth's commodities. God wants our sons to know the surpassing value of an excellent wife.

But how do you get a lanky tween to be interested in such a rare prize?

A boy doesn't develop a desire for a wife quite as naturally as a girl may develop one for a husband. (And that is under attack today too. Don't get me started!) I'd like to suggest a few things that, at the appropriate developmental stages, can help him develop the vision of finding a godly wife.

Use teachable moments to help him see that not all girls are the same. Sound familiar? It's exactly what I advised when we were teaching our boys to be discerning about aggressive girls. At the age of nine or ten, though he probably hasn't met his wife or begun dating, it's important to begin to help him see the difference between an aggressive girl and a good girl.

Just as we take time to talk about the aggressive girls our son encounters—and warn him against them—so should we take time to bring to his attention the good girls our son encounters—and point him toward them. And we should focus on the good girls more than we focus on the aggressive girls because, as I said in *Six Ways to Keep the "Little" in Your Girl*, positive messages are more potent than negative ones.

> Positive messages are more potent than negative ones.

Bob often jokingly told Robby that we'd offer a generous dowry *to* the father of a good woman. He was specific and did this shamelessly. In the presence of everyone in both families. Bob would simply say to the father, "_____ *is a good young woman. What's it going to take to get her to marry my son?"* This often caused Robby to roll his eyes. (Thankfully, he's accustomed to his father's constant trickle of humor and practical jokes and his initial reaction was usually followed by laughter.)

In each case, we'd tell him why this young woman was good. She was a great student. She was into charity work. She was full of laughter. She had the foundation of godly parents. She had the history of a faithful walk with God. These things were discussed often in our home. And I don't think the humor we used to present it hampered the message. Who knows—we may end up paying out one of those dowries! (I sure hope we sell a lot of these books.)

Random Bob Thought: It was funny at the time, but not to Robby.

Bob also used me as an example of the kind of wife Robby should look for. I'm blessed to have a husband who has called me a "good wife" in many ways as we move through family life. When I put a satisfying meal on the table, Bob often says, "Robby, marry well. Your mom is a good cook." When I complete another book, he'll say, "Robby, marry well. Your mom is a good writer." When I find a good bargain, he'll say, "Robby, marry well. Your mom is a good manager of money." He praises my acts of love for the family. Not my looks. Not my personality. My *goodness*.

> **Click here!**
>
> Go to thrivingfamily.com, an online version of Focus on the Family's magazine for parents, and search for "Seven Rules for Dating My Son." These rules offer a lighthearted, practical approach for handling aggressive girls!

If that sounds impossible in your situation, consider this: You can take time to point your son to "good" women like your mother or your pastor's wife. You can even take time to tell him that in face of all the opposition, you're making the decisions you are making because you want to be "good." Be creative. You *can* get this message into his heart!

Introduce your family standards about dating when he's a tween. I shared earlier in the book about a mom who was terribly upset that her eighth-grade son was dating a girl she called a "whore." You may recall that I asked her when she'd shared her standards for dating with him, and she said that it wasn't time yet. But it was. In fact, she'd missed it. It was no wonder that he was dating before she wanted him to, and that he'd not chosen well.

By the time a boy is 11, about a third of his peers are "going out" with someone. (Not sure where they're "going," since they can't drive.) I believe you need to talk to him about your family dating standards before he sees his friends "going out" all around him.

In *Six Ways to Keep the "Little" in Your Girl*, I shared with you our family dating standards, which we introduced to our children when they were in the upper grades of elementary school.

- They are allowed to go on group dates for special events as soon as they hit high school.
- They are allowed to go on single dates when they are 16, as long as we are actively involved in the planning and execution of the evening.
- We discourage them from being exclusive in any relationship until they are out of or nearly out of high school.

It's not a fail-safe plan. Issues of the heart are complicated, but in general we have been pleased with how this plan sets them up to enjoy relationships without the pressure of being in one. It seems to have put the brakes on emotions that could have run away with our kids' spirits in the backseat.

Our goal is that none of them would have a disposable view of relationships. That's what our culture presses upon our kids: "Date…break up…next…date…break up…next…" and so on. Ultimately, this is what we wanted to avoid, so we asked our kids to agree to our family standards before they started in the dating game.

I can't overestimate how critical it is to communicate these standards to your son when he's a tween, even if he doesn't seem interested in girls. It's very easy. Robby more or less said, "Well, okay. Whatever!" It seemed like a nonissue at the time, but a few years down the road, when his heart got entangled in a relationship, our family standards kept it in check. I'm proud of how he's avoided the futility of *many* relationships.

A Man Worthy of Rubies

The church seems a bit imbalanced in how it approaches preparing our children for marriage. There are a great many conversations, teachings, and ministries fostering the Proverbs 31 woman, but what about the Ephesians 5 man? The passage (verses 25-29) admonishes,

Husbands, love your wives, just as Christ loved the church

and gave himself up for her to make her holy, cleansing her by the washing with water through the word, and to present her to himself as a radiant church, without stain or wrinkle or any other blemish, but holy and blameless. In this same way, husbands ought to love their wives as their own bodies. He who loves his wife loves himself. After all, no one ever hated their own body, but they feed and care for their body, just as Christ does the church.

I believe you can begin to build a godly man worthy of a better-than-rubies wife by instilling in him the four character qualities seen in the passage above. (And you'll be building a gentleman to boot!) Let's take a one-by-one-look.

Teach him to give himself up for her by training him to put girls and women first. How does a 12-year-old boy live out Ephesians 5 as he practices the skills of a godly husband? I think he opens the door for you, and he lets you and his sister get in line first for pizza. He carries your daughter's luggage to the car as his dad carries yours.

The next time the culture—or someone at church—takes a swat at your desire to build a gentleman who opens doors for women, you just point them to Ephesians 5:26 and tell them that it was God's idea that a man "lay his life down" for his wife. And that you think one way he can learn that enormous task is to open the door for girls when the opportunity presents itself.

Does this concept make you feel isolated because you aren't experiencing it in your own marriage? My friends Kim and Kerry Michell were in that exact place a few years ago. Then, Kim felt God's Spirit pressing her to be more respectful of her husband. She also knew that he needed to be more of a gentleman toward her. She wanted the two of them to express their masculine and feminine roles to their children in their everyday lives.

Kim respectfully asked Kerry to start doing things like opening the car door for her. She began to listen and be supportive when he made decisions. Their tween son, Christian, *noticed*! He asked his dad, "Why are you opening the car door for Mom all the time?" Kerry told him it was because he wanted to show Kim that he loved her. Imagine the shock, when one rainy Sunday morning Christian insisted she wait inside while he went out to the car to bring in an umbrella so he could escort her out!

Christian isn't acting like a gentleman by putting just his mom first. He knows to put other women first too. He was still a tween when he broke his collarbone. This is an extremely painful injury. Kim and Kerry took him straight to the emergency room, where he began the uncomfortable, painful process of…waiting! While they sat there, an older woman came in for treatment. She was in a wheelchair and just sobbed in pain, even though her injury was far more superficial. Because she was in so much distress, the attendants came to check her to be sure she could wait. Being just like you or me, Kim was about to step into action to ask about her son, when Christian piped up, "Mom, it's okay. I want them to take her first." (Oh yes, he did!)

A man worthy of a better-than-rubies wife is the one who has learned to "give himself up" when he was a tween!

Teach him the Word, and encourage him to share it with others. The picture here is pure first-century Middle-Eastern Jewish tradition. Writing in Ephesians 5, the apostle Paul indicated that the Jewish Old Testament tradition of a bride being bathed and purified in the temple pool no longer applied. Instead, she should be washed every day with the Scriptures brought by her husband. In marriage, this means a husband is called to present the Word of God to his wife and keep her heart clean by doing so. He is in essence charged with the headship of his family's spiritual well-being.

I tire of the testimonial services I attend where a man can't get a word in edgewise because the women are popping up at the speed of light. It's not that I don't believe the women should testify. I just think we get in the way sometimes. We need to give the guys room and allow them time to share. Are we teaching our sons to lead and initiate spiritually when they're in groups of their peers or even adults? Maybe they aren't confident enough in handling the Word to share it. Maybe they aren't steeped enough in prayer to be inspired to share it.

I fell in love with my husband in Sunday-school class. He was my teacher. He knew the Word. My first sense that we'd one day be married came when I found a note in my mailbox applying a Scripture he'd taught to our relationship. That's the kind of guy God says we're supposed to be creating for some precious girl out there—a man who knows the Word and can share it with others.

Random Bob Thought:
That was a good move!
I married well!

Get your son into AWANA, Boys' Brigade, and other great Bible-memory programs before he's a tween. Hide that Word in his heart as much as you can. Then, during his tween years, find ways for him to deepen his faith in father–son Bible study, Sunday-school class, and youth group. Teach him the Word.

As he progresses, share with him his calling to be able to lead his family in the Word. Help him practice that by applying the verses and concepts he's learning to everyday situations. When his friend is sad because his faithful dog died, encourage your son to find a scripture to send to him. When his team loses and they have a bad attitude, challenge him to find a verse that would have helped them respond better. When he doesn't feel like studying, share with him a verse that urges him to do his best. These little acts prepare him to share the Word with his wife and his children one day. (After all, most of the time we're just communicating to our spouse and children in the way we saw it modeled in our homes, right?) You can't really control whether his heart stays yielded to this, but you can give him a good head start!

Remind him often that the purity of any of his relationships with women is his responsibility, not theirs, and define the boundaries clearly for him. While many of the topics I've addressed in this book encourage your son to live a life of personal purity, this is the first time I've addressed the teaching that the purity of his wife…and other men's future wives he may date before he finds his wife…is *his* responsibility. Nowhere in Scripture does God specifically tell the woman she is responsible to present a man without spot or wrinkle, but our sons are clearly presented with the example of Christ. They are ultimately the ones who answer to God for the purity of their wives. This is probably not a concept you'll introduce until after his tweens, but it's worth noting since it should happen early in his teens.

In order for your son to be successful, you'll need to help him answer the question, *How far is too far?* The blunt truth is that if we don't clearly define the lines, they'll get crossed simply because an aroused guy has a hard time slowing things down once the engine is revved up. (Yep, I'm talking about our sons. Let's get real and own up to the fact that, while we will always see that sweet footed-pajama three-year-old, our sons grow into hot-blooded teens…and just like the ones some of us wish we'd never dated, if they aren't taught boundaries.)

In *Who Moved the Goalpost?*, Bob wrote about the stages of physical intimacy. I've included them in the sidebar on the next page so you can introduce them to your son when he's about 14. Yep,

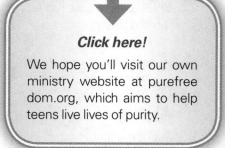

Click here!

We hope you'll visit our own ministry website at purefree dom.org, which aims to help teens live lives of purity.

there are some really tough subjects on this list, but we both believe that a parent has to address things like oral sex and masturbation or your son will be vulnerable to the world's standards, and they won't line up with your desires for him to live a life of purity. The world says that if you get to your wedding night disease-free and without an unwanted pregnancy, you've succeeded. God says that there should not be even a *hint* of sexual sin in your son's life (Ephesians 5:3).

And that it's his job to make sure the same is true for the girls he dates.

Cultivate in him a desire to feed and care for his future wife and family by building a solid work ethic in him. While a wife may contribute to a

How far will you go?

1. Looking at a girl and making eye contact. (Guys are visually stimulated.)
2. Talking with a girl. (Hey, ever notice how much passion talk can create?)
3. Holding hands. (This can be a nice sign of attachment.)
4. Hands on shoulders and hands on waist. (Can you handle this? Can she?)
5. Kissing on the cheek or softly kissing on the lips. (This is a sweet, innocent kiss.)
6. Open-mouthed passionate kissing. (A new desire awakens.)
7. Petting while clothed.
8. Mutual masturbation.
9. Oral sex.
10. Sexual intercourse.

family income, it's in a man's DNA to be a provider. If he's not successful at this, it can cause a lot of strain in the marriage.

How does a tween prepare to feed and care for his future wife? By being a student who "studies to show himself approved." By working as hard as he can to assist his dad in yardwork and taking out the trash. By getting a paper route on the weekend until he's older and can take it on through the weekdays.

One of my greatest rewards in mothering Robby came when he was a sophomore in college. I'd noticed that a lot of his friends in college were in dating relationships. I wondered if that bothered my boy, so I asked! He told me he didn't have a lot of time given the rigor of his academic program, but he was working hard now so he could care for the right woman when he met her. (Be. Still. My. Heart.)

Keep Swimming Upstream

Many of the moms who spoke into the content of this book expressed a desire to raise godly, pure sons of honor who would find godly wives so they could create beautiful families. But many of them also stated that they felt very lonely in that calling—and overwhelmed by the peer pressure. One expressed it very well when she said,

It saddens me, and I feel like we go 10 steps ahead at home

and 20 steps behind at school. Never can get ahead of what the peers are showing him and teaching him already at this age. Worrying about jr. high for next year and even considering homeschooling. Feel like no matter what we do, we are going to fail because the peer pressure is so high. Things that I remember starting in high school are now starting in grade school. Times have changed, but my husband and I haven't and will not allow it, but how do we keep our kids protected from it?

Will your son's value system be chipped away at by his peers? Yes! Recently I was telling Robby how grateful I am that he occasionally helps me drive his high-school sisters around when I can't. Since he lives in town, I'll call him if I need a late-night pickup for Autumn from an away basketball game, or if I can't make it to get Lexi from drama class. He never says no, and he's always cheerful about helping. I was shocked by what he said one time when I asked whether he minded my requests:

> Robby: *"I don't mind at all, but my friends mind."*
>
> Me: *"What do you mean?"*
>
> Robby: *"Some of them tell me I should be angry that you call me. They don't want me to miss the basketball game or stop playing PlayStation with them."*
>
> Me: *"What do you tell them?"*
>
> Robby: *"That I have 20,000 reasons to say yes."*

I smile knowingly, realizing he means the $20,000 we're trying to help him come up with each year for college tuition.

Do you know what I hear in that boy's words? A grateful gentleman. He doesn't mind helping. He's not focused on "me." He's putting his own desires to the side to help his sisters, and to show appreciation to Bob and me for our sacrifices.

And...

He's surviving peer pressure!

The peer pressure is strong, and it may require you to take drastic action to protect your value system, but don't give up. It is possible. My son has turned out "good."

Years ago, when she and I were releasing the book *Lies Young Women Believe*, Nancy Leigh DeMoss delivered an amazing impromptu address to an audience of teen girls who felt like they could barely survive the peer pressure around them. She simply said, "Be salmon!"

Salmon swim upstream.

You'll feel that way a lot if you parent a man child to be a godly gentleman who desires to care for a wife and children.

But keep swimming upstream anyway!

His Way

What are your family dating standards? Write them below. Discuss them with your husband. Make it a goal to set aside a time to share these with your son before he's in middle school.

Also take time to pray through how you are specifically demonstrating your expectations that your son be a gentleman. Ask God to give you some creative ideas. Write your goals below.

_____

_____

_____

_____

_____

_____

_____

_____

_____

_____

_____

_____

_____

_____

_____

Prayer

Lord, we seem to be living in an era when people love themselves more than they love their families. Nor do we love goodness anymore. Forgive us. Please let my family be different. Help us to honor your plan for family and mankind. Instill in us a love for family. Specifically, I pray that my son, _____, will be a young man who has an uncommon love for family, both the one he is in now and the one he will build as a good man. May he have true godliness in his life, and may the power of that godliness be evidenced in his goodness. In Jesus' Name, amen!

"The one thing I did right in raising my boys was praying for wisdom and for the Lord to make good, not harm, come of any parenting mistakes."

Jackie Stauffer, mother to
Ryan, 22, and Derek, 18

Fast-Forward Ten Years

O ne round-trip ticket to Austria, please!
  Gulp.

As I finish up this book, my son is about to turn 21. And he's going to do it 5324.94 miles away from home. (Not that I calculated it or anything.) In just a few weeks, he'll be boarding a plane to Vienna, Austria, where he's taking a class in German. I'm not sure how I'll handle the goodbye, but I do know there will need to be a bucket for my tears.

Robby's looming departure reminds me of another time when I hugged him goodbye at an airport, exactly ten years ago. When he was 11, Bob and I were sending him off to Florida to meet his two best friends (twins) for a week of summer fun. Just as he boarded the plane, the TV screens in the airport began blaring news of shark attacks off the coast of Florida. "Summer of the Shark" read the words moving across the screen. I burst into tears and prayed the whole way home. It is a mother's heart desire to keep her children close—when they are tweens and when they are young adults. But they won't always be nearby for us to guide and protect.

And it's not the sharks of this world we need to worry about.

It's the stinkin' Tree.

The Tree...Again

You'll recall that we ran up against the Tree early in the book. We suggested that the complacency Adam brought to his and Eve's encounter with the Tree of the Knowledge of Good and Evil led to a lot of badness for all of us. If only Adam had stepped up to be good...useful and strong. Instead, he got boring, passive, and filled with the flesh. What a sad day for our Great Father! I think I have a small sense of how that felt for our big, living, loving God. As our children dig their teeth into the "apples" of this world, we can go from feeling as big as the universe to as small as a pebble in an instant.

Recently, I've watched my very good son struggle with complacency over a big life choice. There was no evil, ill intent, or rebellion in the boy. Just a lot of casual acceptance of how things were rolling along. But the eyes of wise parents can see past the decisions of a young adult to the consequences that will be felt for decades down the road. My eyes burned with tears as I looked through the lenses of "what if?" My stomach churned with pleading for him to rise up and be good. I learned that sometimes the worse rebellion is standing at the base of the Tree and doing nothing. What hopelessness I felt for a short season of my son's well-lived life.

Did God feel like that when Adam stood at the base of the Tree and did nothing?

Let me be clear: Adam sinned terribly. He chose it. It changed the course of not only his life, but ours. But for a brief moment just before he bit into that fruit, his sin was rather quiet. It was one of complacency. He just wanted to go along with the flow that Satan had initiated and Eve had begun to follow. His complacency led to rebellion.

Every day our children do perfectly "normal" things that go along with the flow of this world's brokenness, and it leads to rebellion.

It would be good to note that the Tree was not evil. It was created by God and it was good, but the timing of partaking, the simple fact that God had forbidden it, and the lack of self-control in the face of temptation were what made it an act of rebellion.

The Tree comes in many forms. When our children are four, it could show up as a toy that's not theirs but they have to have it—so they throw a tantrum, thus "biting the apple." When they are tweens, the Tree could show up as popularity—so they complacently ignore a worthy friend when they pick teams at recess, thus "biting the apple." When they are teens, the Tree could show up as an aggressive girl—so they complacently throw your advice to the wind and "go out" under the radar, thus "biting the apple."

As they become young adults that Tree looms larger than it ever has before. It shows up in their career path...the way they embrace their faith...their pursuit of marriage. The stakes are much higher than they once were. The tiniest bit of complacency can lead to rebellion that will change the course of their lives.

And then there's the matter of family legacy—the good and the bad—to throw into the mix. The fruit that's been born from the family tree makes it either easier or harder for our children to say "no" when a snake slithers around the fruit calling their name.

You know how the Tree shows up in your house.

I know how it shows up in mine.

The fact is this: It *does* show up.

The Tree is in Austria.

And I know it.

I know nothing specific about what temptations my son will face there. I have no specific reason to be alarmed. In fact, I believe only great things about his opportunities there, and he has proven himself to be good. Here are some specific ways he blesses my heart and proves his goodness. (And if you have a 20-year-old, you'll know how big these are.)

- His teenage sisters know they can count on him if they need a ride somewhere...or help with math. (He is patient.)

- He drove his friend Caleb to Fort Jackson, South Carolina, when he needed a ride. (He is faithful.)

- He's the one—out of four very good roommates—who takes the time to manage the rent, and he volunteers to run PowerPoint at church. (He is helpful.)

- He works hard to maintain his position in an honors program at Penn State. (He is diligent.)

- He never brags about his GPA, and I often see him hide his achievement. (He is humble.)

I guess what I'm saying is this: Goodness shows up in the little things. Not *just* the big stuff. And I know that my son is displaying goodness in his actions and choices. The reward of our being faithful during his tween years is being seen as we launch him into his adult life.

But the world is not all good.

It's filled with temptation like that encountered at the base of the Tree.

That's why, as I enter this season of releasing my son, I'm arming myself with prayer. And it's why you also should do most of your strategy sessions for building a good boy on your knees in your prayer closet.

Last night Bob and I gathered with our dear friends Pastor Jonathan and Suzy Weibel, and we prayed about that Tree as it shows up for their young adult children and ours. As I pondered our sweet prayer time this morning, I found some comfort reading from Genesis 3. In a way I'd never seen it before, I saw how God responded to his own children when they succumbed to the Tree.

In short: He chased his son and his daughter down and picked a fight!

Why It's Okay to Fight

Oh, to be sure, those two kids—Adam and Eve were their names—hid from him when they heard his footsteps. (Have you ever seen your child "hide"? Maybe when they were very small and knew they'd done something bad they hid behind a sofa. Maybe now that they're older they have given you the silent treatment or you've seen them try to hide the truth. It's human nature to hide when we taste the fruit of the Tree.) The strong Father does not give up on them, but bellows,

> *"Where are you?"*

This morning when I read it, it sounded a little more like

> *"Just where do you think YOU are going?!"*

In my mind, it had the strength of a Father showing up several hours after a mom had said, "Just wait until your father shows up!" It reeked of warning. To be sure there would be punishment ahead.

And then…whoa! Talk about your time-out. God brings out the whoop-butt on these two kids and serves up physical pain, emotional drama, a little bit of hard labor, and a death sentence to make sure they learn their lesson well. Then, as if sending them to their room for solitary confinement, he kicks them out of the garden. (And, if you know the rest of the story, he sacrifices his very self to restore the relationship and its joys. Kind of reminds me of the times I've told my kids, "This is going to hurt me more than it's going to hurt you.")

Here's the point: I was comforted by the fact that the original family survived an awfully big family fight. It means mine can too. Please understand, I'm not talking about "yelling" at your son or harming him emotionally or physically. I'm talking about taking a stand when he gets too close to that Tree! Perhaps *conflict* is a better word to use than *fighting*. But in our house it feels like *fighting*. At least that word is more descriptive of the emotional toll it takes on this mom's heart when unity is broken, even for the sake of righteousness. (Maybe that's why God made our husbands to be Wolf Dads. They take the fighting a little better than we do.)

Out of the 17 books I've written, *Six Ways to Keep the "Little" in Your Girl* and this one have been the most emotionally draining for me. Why? Because our family is full of drama. We are often fighting to keep the "little" and the "good" in our family. We pick fights when our kids reach for the Tree. I don't like it.

But you know what?

It's okay.

It's okay to share conflict together.

In fact, it's a good sign. In his encouragement to let conflict happen, Dr. Edward Hallowell writes,

> *There is conflict in connected families. In fact, the presence of conflict is a good indicator that there is a connection.* [1]

I want peace and harmony as much as the next girl. But the right kind of conflict is a good sign. It means we care. We would not have conflict if we didn't care. And we would not care if we weren't connected.

"You Belong to the Lord"

Throughout this book, I've shared the wisdom of Angela Thomas with you. May I just say that our conversation together was like a Z-Pak for the sickness in my prayer life? This sweet woman is strong in every way, especially in her faith-filled conversation with our Mighty Savior. She specifically encouraged me in this area of conflict with our children. As we began to discuss it she said,

> *When you confront your kids, you know they're going to roll their eyes. They might even spit! At the end of the day I'm like, "Who cares!? I'm the MOTHER! I have to be accountable to God for how I've protected you. And I'm way more scared of God than I am of you!"*

Doesn't that just resurrect the courage in your mother's heart?

She went on to share a time that her teenage son, Grayson, really stuffed his emotions about her failed marriage, and as a result withdrew in every way humanly possible. This one took the road of the prodigal—not in open rebellion, but in emotional distancing. He simply stuffed all his emotions, and when he was full enough to burst he simply shut down. At the end of all her protection, her then-14-year-old decided to go live with his father. Can you imagine the hurt?

But Angela didn't let the hurt fester. She used it to fuel her faith.

> *Every time Grayson would come and visit, we would all gather around him as a family and we'd hug him. I would say, "Baby, you feel this?" He'd mumble, "Yeeaaah" in a low, unemotional voice.*
>
> *"Do you know I love you?"*
>
> *"Yeeaah."*
>
> *"Do you know I'm praying my heart out for you?"*
>
> *"Yeeahh."*
>
> *"Alright, baby. You belong to the Lord."*

This is a mom who would not back down from both demanding righteous behavior…and loving unconditionally. That's good conflict! The kind that demands good living. Good character.

Nearly everyone had given up on Grayson. It looked like nothing was happening in his overstuffed heart of hurt. But Angela kept praying and giving him to the Lord. Then one day he called. He had given his life to the Lord. And with his heart full of emotion he said, "Mom, God told me to come home!"

"Pack it up, baby. We're comin' to get ya!" rejoiced Angela.

As she recounted this story to me she said,

> *His eyes were different. You could see it now. Before, it was hard to see the hand of the Lord. I had to trust it was there. The Holy Spirit is doing things in our kids' lives even when we can't see it. When I look at Grayson—he's in the room next to me as we speak and he's winning his community for Christ these days—I say, "Who* doesn't *believe in God?" I want to show them this boy who did a complete 180! I just want to testify to the alive power and redeeming work of my Lord. I know there will be more times I have to trust my God because I can't see His hand, but my kids will be okay. They belong to God.*

That fuels my heart. Does it yours?

Grayson is good.

He is looking outside of his own desires and needs in order to bring his community to the foot of the cross. It doesn't get any "gooder" than that!

Whatever your circumstances as you read this, it *is* possible to raise a good son in today's me-centered culture. It *is* possible to build a son who embraces self-control, honor, responsibility, purpose, community, purity, integrity, and family love. But there will be bumps along the way—and that's when a connecting mom embraces the hope that's in every family conflict. She does this by standing her ground…and hitting her knees.

At the end of the day, it always comes down to Psalm 127:1 for me:

Unless the LORD builds the house, its builders labor in vain.

In *Six Ways to Keep the "Little" in Your Girl*, I shared that this verse would be more accurately translated if it read, "Unless the Lord *repairs* the house, its builders labor in vain."

Truly, our children belong to the Lord, and it's our job to hand them back to him again and again for much-needed repairs. In fact, why don't you do that right now? Insert the names of your family members into this prayer:

Lord, build and repair my home heart by heart. Build and repair me. Build and repair _____, _____, and _____. Do not let my labor as a mother be in vain!

As you labor to keep the "good" in your boy, don't let it be in vain. Stay in constant communion with the Lord, be obedient to his nudges, and never grow faithless when it looks hopeless. Remember, your son belongs to the Lord.

It has been our prayer as you read this book that you would experience no sense of guilt for how you have chosen to parent. (Guilt says, "I'm bad!") Our hope is that as you've prayed the prayers in this book, you've had moments of sensing a sweet spirit of conviction. (Conviction says, "I'm waaaayyy too good for this!") Grasp that truth. Hold on to it. God calls *you*…not just your son…to His goodness.

Whoever seeks good finds favor.

Proverbs 11:27

Seeing the Gift of ADD and ADHD

by Bob Gresh

I was a rather bright kid. I read so much that my mom had to nag me to go outside to play. In school, my grades were good. Other than being the class clown, I didn't seem to have any early signs that I was going to face some special challenges in life. Then, the leaf collection was due.

And past due.

And then some.

My patient, loving teacher kept asking me to hand it in. Fall became winter. And there were no leaves. Winter became spring and the leaves came back, and so did a new deadline for my project.

Finally, that bighearted teacher told me she'd just pass me anyway.

That was the first time I felt paralyzed by something.

And it would happen again and again.

The worst experience was my senior project in college. That time the deadline knocked me right off my feet and put me in bed for a day with depression.

I just couldn't seem to pull together those extra big assignments.

It wasn't until several years into our marriage that our dear counselor, Tippy Duncan, gave me a name for what ailed me: Attention Deficit Disorder.

Fast-forward 20 years. I am a Christian high school administrator. In 2004 I founded a special kind of Christian school (see www.graceprep.com for more info). It's different for a lot of reasons. One of them is that the guy with ADD is running it rather than trying to survive as a student. Although we've produced a National Merit Scholar, several Ivy-League-level college students, and a whole lot of other academic achievements, I'd like to think that one of our greatest achievements is providing a safe, unique environment for students who, like me, struggle with ADD/ADHD.

Over the years I've come to appreciate my ADD. And I'm oftentimes deeply depressed by it also. ADD is not just being hyperactive. It's been documented that there are several different types. Each type can result in unique challenges such as anxiety, depression, lack of focus, compulsivity, impulsivity, angry outbursts, and a tendency toward obsessive or addictive behaviors. These are very real biochemical problems. I know. I've seen pictures of my brain. It doesn't look like Dannah's, and if you don't have ADD it doesn't look like yours (see the next page). That's why it might be hard for you to understand if you're living with a son who is different like I am.

Must-reads for the ADD family

There are many books on the subject of ADD and many experts, but here are a few that even I as an ADD reader can get through and enjoy:

- *Driven to Distraction* by Edward M. Hallowell (a must-read!)
- *Healing ADD: The Breakthrough Program That Allows You to See and Heal the 6 Types of ADD* by Daniel Amen
- *ADD-Friendly Ways to Organize Your Life* by Judith Kolberg and Kathleen Nadeau

Because of my own personal challenges with ADD and how it affects our lives, Dannah and I have read a multitude of books on the topic. Here are the key points we feel you should consider.

1. Generally, ADD has been and tends to be overdiagnosed. As real as it is, sadly, it's also a label stuck on boys who just haven't had enough time outside, or who have had too much time in front of an Xbox, or who have been eating nothing but carbs and processed food. From a historical perspective, kids are as sedentary today as they've ever been, perhaps more so. Before you jump to ADD as a diagnosis, try some healthy eating habits and daily exercise. See if your son gets some focus from it. If he does, be thankful and move on.

2. ADD is real, documentable, and treatable just like any other physical challenge. Dr. Daniel Amen is one of the pioneers in diagnosing and helping families with ADD (for more info, see www.amenclinics.com). His methods are in the vanguard, and in many medical fields practitioners have been slow to embrace them, but they have. Amen says that it is optimal to look at a brain before you diagnose it. (Kind of like looking at an X-ray of a possibly broken bone.)

I have had my brain scanned twice. Both times gave me a more specific diagnosis. I can see my ADD in the scan below just like you could see a tumor in a lung or a broken bone. It's real.

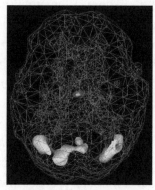
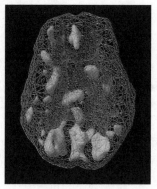

Scan of the average active brain.

Scan of Bob's ADD brain when active.

Provided by Amen Clinics, amenclinics.com.

Dr. Amen has identified six different types of ADD. Each has its own set of challenges and requires a very distinct treatment regimen for the sufferer to operate successfully in life.

3. Treatment can make life much easier for the entire family. The most controversial part of ADD is medication. I would say this: When an adult has high blood pressure, high cholesterol, or ulcers in the stomach there seems to be little question that medication can help such maladies. And yet the one area of the body for which the general public, and Christians in particular, stigmatize medication is the brain. When a doctor prescribes meds below the neck, all is well. When he prescribes them above the neck, it creates stigma, embarrassment, and arguments.

I know the benefits of proper medication. And I also know several downsides of improper medication. For years I was not aware there were different types of ADD, and I allowed myself to be treated presumptively by physicians who lumped all ADD sufferers into one big category. After simply reading Daniel Amen's book *Healing ADD*, we quickly identified my type, and medication became much more effective. It is still an ongoing process of evaluation to keep my brain chemicals balanced, but having an accurate diagnosis has made a huge difference.

> ### Practical-living help for ADD
>
> Amen Clinics offers a fantastic website for those with the challenge of ADD, as well as anyone hoping to improve the functionality of their brain. You'll find eating advice, exercise tips, fun games that actually improve thinking ability, and much more at theamensolution.com.

4. Exercise and nutrition are as powerful as medicine. Though I have not been able to live successfully without medication for a number of years, I have found that when I combine medication with exercise and nutrition I am my most focused and happiest. Most ADD types live best on a higher-protein, low-carb diet.

I am very transparent about my struggles and how I deal with them. If I didn't have Eileen, my wonder assistant, and didn't have my iPhone beeping every time I need to be at the next place, I would not get to the next place. Obviously students don't have the advantage of either of these things. Often they need a parent to help them along paths that would probably be easy for other children. We know of one parent who found that flash cards on a Rolodex in the bathroom ensured that her ADD child would come down for breakfast fully dressed, with hair brushed and teeth brushed, and with his backpack for school. Without the cards, mornings were stressful and filled with anxiety. In doing this loving act, the parents were teaching him to live—like I do today—with a list constantly in front of him. This keeps me focused and on task also. Without it, I am lost.

At times I'd like to be normal and have normal brain patterns, but in many cases I can celebrate my different way of thinking. It has allowed me to excel in certain areas, think outside the box, break paradigms, and make my life and the lives of those around me extremely interesting. (Read: chaos!) Seriously, the reason I was and am the class clown is because I have a limitless reservoir of ideas and creativity. (That, in itself, has its challenges, and Dannah sometimes has to tell me to just stop having ideas for the day!) Here are the names of some famous people who have or are thought to have had ADD:

- Abraham Lincoln, United States president
- Ludwig van Beethoven, composer
- Alexander Graham Bell, inventor
- Ansel Adams, photographer
- Jim Carrey, comedian
- Winston Churchill, statesman
- Walt Disney, entrepreneur
- F. Scott Fitzgerald, author
- Magic Johnson, basketball player

Some of our greatest inventors, artists, and musicians have had ADD and didn't do well in the public-school format we currently have. (Winston Churchill failed sixth grade.) But they went on to live successfully.

And so have I.

And your son can too.

Notes

Chapter 1—Is There a Mouse in That Cookie Box?

1. John Tierney, "Adultescent," *New York Times*, December 26, 2004, accessed at HighBeam .com February 2, 2011.

2. Kay. S. Hymowitz, *Manning Up: How the Rise of Women Has Turned Men into Boys* (New York: Basic Books, 2011), 2.

3. Book review of Joe Carmichiel, *Permanent Adolescence: Why Boys Don't Grow Up* (Far Hills, NJ: New Horizon Press, 2008), posted at HighBeam.com August 19, 2009,

4. Sharon Jayson, "More college hookups, but more virgins, too," *USA Today*, March 31, 2010.

5. Robert Coles, *The Moral Intelligence of Children* (New York: Plume/Penguin, 1998), 22.

6. Michael Gurian, *The Wonder of Boys* (New York: Tarcher/Putnam, 1997), xvii.

7. Gurian, xix.

8. Coles, 17.

Chapter 2—A Mom's Greatest Fears

1. http://yourlife.usatoday.com/parenting-family/teen-ya/story/2011-09-03/Close-bond-with-mom-helps-keep-teen-boys-safe/50250408/1.

2. Dave Gardner, "What's troubling the BOYS?" *Northeast Pennyslvania Business Journal*, February 1, 2010, accessed at HighBeam.com February 2011.

3. Tony Dokoupil, "Why I Am Leaving Guyland," *Newsweek*, September 8, 2008, accessed at HighBeam.com February 2011.

4. Michael Gurian, *The Purpose of Boys* (San Francisco: Jossey-Bass, 2010), 124.

5. "Study: More Kids Exposed to Online Porn," AP Online, February 5, 2007, accessed at High Beam.com February 2011.

6. Kay S. Hymowitz, *Manning Up: How the Rise of Women Has Turned Men into Boys* (New York: Basic Books, 2011), 14.

7. Mike Snider, "Nielsen: Spending on video games outpaces print and home video," *USA Today*, February 25, 2010, accessed at usatoday.com April 2, 2010.

8. Gurian, 125.

9. Michael Thompson, "Understanding the world of boys from 8 to 10," *Work and Family Life*, June 1, 2008, accessed at HighBeam.com February 2011.

10. Nicolas A. Roes, "Embrace the angry young man," *Addiction Professional*, September 1, 2008, accessed at HighBeam.com February 2011.

11. National Highway Traffic Safety Administration, 2005 FARS (Fatality Analysis Reporting System Encyclopedia) data.

12. Roes.

Chapter 3—Becoming a Connecting Mom

1. Edward M. Hallowell, *The Childhood Roots of Adult Happiness* (New York: Ballantine Books, 2003), 172.

Chapter 4—Why Connecting Matters

1. Amanda Onion, "Parent-Child Connection Shapes Brain," ABCnews.com, December 5, 2005.
2. Joe S. McIlhaney Jr. and Freda McKissic Bush, *Hooked: New Science on How Casual Sex Is Affecting Our Children* (Chicago: Northfield Publishing, 2008), 53.
3. McIlhaney and Bush.

Chapter 6—Warning: Male Brain on Testosterone Straight Ahead

1. Nate Larkin, *Samson and the Pirate Monks: Calling Men to Authentic Brotherhood* (Nashville, TN: Thomas Nelson, 2006), xi.

Chapter 7—Way #1: Get Him Outside to Play

1. Alan F. Lambert, "Reconnecting Kids and the Outdoors," Congressional testimony, May 24, 2007, accessed at HighBeam.com February 2011.
2. An estimated 40 percent of all elementary schools have eliminated or are in the process of eliminating recess. Some claim this is about time management. In James Dobson's bestseller *Bringing Up Boys,* protecting recess for children is one of the points he strongly advocates, because it's critical to a child's developing mind.
3. "VOA News: Parents Urged to Let Children Play Outside," US Fed News Services, May 21, 2007, accessed at HighBeam.com February 2011.
4. Conn Iggulden and Hal Iggulden, *The Dangerous Book for Boys* (New York: Collins, 2007), 110.
5. Iggulden and Iggulden, 1.
6. Shaunti Feldhahn and Lisa A. Rice, *For Parents Only* (Colorado Springs, CO: Multnomah, 2007), 67.

Chapter 8—Way #2: Give Him a Book So He Can Discover a Real "Call of Duty"

1. "Widening Academic Gap Paints Sobering Picture For Boys: From Kindergarten to College, Boys Are Getting Their Lunch Handed to Them by Girls," *Portland Press Herald*, April 1, 2006, accessed at HighBeam.com February 2011.
2. Joan Garrett, "Gap Between College Men and Women Persists," *Chattanooga Times Free Press*, March 25, 2010, accessed at HighBeam.com February, 2011.
3. *Portland Press Herald*.
4. Dennis and Barbara Rainey, *"Parenting Today's Adolescent: Helping Your Child Avoid the Traps of the Preteen and Teen Years* (Nashville, TN: Thomas Nelson, 1998), 274.
5. "Effects of Technology and Male Teachers on Boys' Reading," *Australian Journal of Education*, April 1, 2008, accessed at HighBeam.com February 2011.
6. Edward M. Hallowell, *The Childhood Roots of Adult Happiness* (New York: Ballantine Books, 2003), 172.
7. Michael Gurian, *The Wonder of Boys* (New York: Tarcher/Putnam, 1997), 11.
8. John Eldredge, *Wild at Heart* (Nashville, TN: Thomas Nelson, 2001), 6, 7.
9. Thomas Spence, "How to Raise Boys to Read," *Wall Street Journal*, September 24, 2010, accessed at online.wsj.com February 5, 2011.
10. Gurian, notepad.

Chapter 9—Way #3: Host Wing Nites and Fantasy Football Parties

1. Meg Meeker, *Boys Should Be Boys: 7 Secrets To Raising Healthy Sons* (New York, Ballantine Books, 2009), 1, 2.

2. "Wolfing" is a concept introduced to us by Kay Briscoe King of Texas. Kay was a counselor to Bob Gresh during his early years of marriage, and the concept of "wolfing" deeply impacted the entire Gresh family.

Chapter 10—Way #4: Celebrate His Entrance into Manhood

1. Eric Sigel, "Puberty for Boys," Clinical Reference Systems, January 1, 2000, accessed at High Beam.com February 2011.

Chapter 11—Way #5: Unplug Him from a Plugged-In World

1. Jim Taylor, *Your Children Under Attack: How Popular Culture Is Destroying Your Kids' Values, and How You Can Protect Them* (Naperville, IL: Sourcebooks, Inc., 2005), 19.

2. "Study: More Kids Exposed to Online Porn," AP Online, February 5, 2007, accessed at High Beam.com February 2011.

3. Penny Marshall, "Poisoned by Porn," *Daily Mail* (London, England), March 6, 2010, accessed at HighBeam.com January 15, 2011.

4. www.planetcrush.org/Images/Media/news_mypaper250110.pdf, accessed July 15, 2011.

5. As delivered in a message broadcast on Focus on the Family's daily program, April 5, 2011, accessed via Focus on the Family's iPhone application April 7, 2011.

6. Ed Young, *Pure Sex* (Sisters, OR: Multnomah, 1997), 18.

7. Juliet B. Schor, *Born to Buy* (New York: Scribner, 2004), 20.

8. Micah White, "Screen Addiction," adbusters.com, May 21, 2009, accessed April 7, 2011.

9. Jay Giedd, interview on PBS Frontline, "Inside the Teenage Brain: The Wiring of the Adolescent Brain," accessed at www.pbs.org/wgbh/pages/frontline/shows/teenbrain/interviews/giedd.html September 2011.

Chapter 12—Way #6: Let Him Open the Car Door for You

1. Leonard Sax, *Boys Adrift: The Five Factors Driving the Growing Epidemic of Unmotivated Boys and Underachieving Young Men* (New York: Basic Books, 2007), 164.

2. Sax, 166.

Conclusion—Fast-Forward Ten Years

1. Edward M. Hallowell, *The Childhood Roots of Adult Happiness* (New York: Ballantine Books, 2003), 172.

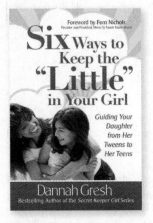

Six Ways to Keep the "Little" in Your Girl

Guiding Your Daughter from Her Tweens to Her Teens

Dannah Gresh

Today's world pressures girls to act older than they are when they're not ready for it. How can you help your tween daughter navigate the stormy waters of boy-craziness, modesty, body image, media, Internet safety, and more?

Dannah Gresh shares six easy ways to help your daughter grow up to be confident, emotionally healthy, and strong in her faith. In a warm and transparent style, Dannah shows you how to

- help your daughter celebrate her body in a healthy way
- unbrand her when the world tries to buy and sell her
- unplug her from a plugged-in world
- dream with her about her future

"A practical, biblically based resource to navigate the rapids of raising a tween girl...Even better, this book is fun to read—more like eating dark chocolate than eating broccoli. Enjoy!"

Dr. Juli Slattery
Family psychologist, Focus on the Family

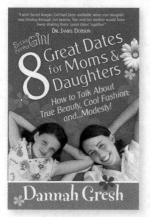

8 GREAT DATES FOR MOMS AND DAUGHTERS

How to Talk About True Beauty, Cool Fashion, and…Modesty!

DANNAH GRESH

One of the greatest protections against the culture's push to make your daughter mature too quickly is quality connecting time with you. Dannah Gresh, popular speaker and creator of Secret Keeper Girl live events and resources, has developed this mom–daughter "date" book to help you replace our culture's lies with truth and make a lasting connection with your tween girl.

This new and updated version contains the simple plans for eight fun activities to share (think facials, tea parties, shopping challenges!). Perfect for you and your energetic 8- to 12-year-old, each date helps you answer real-life questions like—

- "What is real beauty?"
- "How can I feel okay about my body?"
- "*Why* do I have to dress modestly?"
- "How do I take care of my hair?"

You'll find proven methods to bring up a healthy, grounded, and spiritually whole girl!

> "I wish Secret Keeper Girl had been available when our daughter was moving through her tweens. She and her mother would have loved sharing these 'great dates' together."
>
> *Dr. James Dobson*

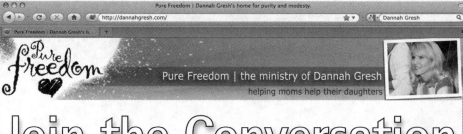

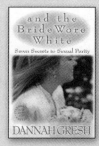

More Great Resources from Harvest House

52 THINGS KIDS NEED FROM A MOM

What Mothers Can Do to Make a Lifelong Difference
ANGELA THOMAS

Angela Thomas, bestselling author and mother of four, draws on personal experience and biblical principles to help you raise healthy, responsible children and establish strong family ties. Whether you have one baby or six growing kids, insightful stories and practical information cover childhood through the teen years and are packed with specifics to help you...

- establish a positive, wholesome atmosphere at home
- make your children feel loved and secure
- teach and encourage communication
- know when and how to correct behavior and set consequences
- help your kids persevere and succeed

52 Things Kids Need from a Mom will help you discover God's wisdom for moms in a way that's upbeat and guilt-free!

52 THINGS KIDS NEED FROM A DAD

What Fathers Can Do to Make a Lifelong Difference
JAY PAYLEITNER

Good news—you are already the perfect dad for your kids! Still, you know you can grow. In these pages, Jay Payleitner, veteran radio producer and dad of five, offers a bounty of inspiring and unexpected insights:

- *straightforward rules*: "carry photos of your kids," "dad tucks in," and "kiss your wife in the kitchen"
- *candid advice that may be tough to hear*: "get right with

your own dad," "throw out your porn," and "surrender control of the TV remote"

- *weird topics that at first seem absurd*: "buy Peeps," "spin a bucket over your head," and "rent a dolphin"

Surely, God—our heavenly Father—designed fatherhood to be a joy, a blessing, and a blast!

THE MOM I WANT TO BE

Rising Above Your Past to Give Your Kids a Great Future
T. SUZANNE ELLER

Your experience as a mother—and a woman—is influenced by the mothering you received as a child. If neglect or inconsistency was a part of your upbringing, you need a healthy vision of the wonderful thing motherhood can be. From her own difficult experience, Suzie Eller shows you...

- how shattered legacies can be put back together
- ways to forgive, let go, and leave your parenting baggage in the past
- how to give your kids the gift of good memories and a great future

With Suzie, you'll celebrate God's healing power...and all that can and will be done in your life as you become the mom you want to be.